The Man Who Saved FC Barcelona

The Remarkable Life of Patrick O'Connell

SUE O'CONNELL

AMBERLEY

All of the major events in this book, and most of the minor ones, are true. For the sake of narrative flow, one or two of the minor events have been altered slightly. The conversations are as authentic as possible, given that no one knows precisely what was said. The newspaper extracts have been paraphrased by the author from articles of the time.

First published 2016

Amberley Publishing
The Hill, Stroud
Gloucestershire, GL5 4EP

www.amberley-books.com

British Library Cataloguing in Publication Data.
A catalogue record for this book is available from the British Library.

ISBN 978 1 4456 5468 3 (print)
ISBN 978 1 4456 5469 0 (ebook)

Maps by Thomas Bohm, User Design.
Typesetting and Origination by Amberley Publishing.

Printed and bound in Great Britain by
Marston Book Services Ltd, Oxfordshire

Contents

Contents

Contents

Foreword

When I first received a phone call at the PFA offices from Fergus Dowd in August 2014, little did I realise it would take me on a very, very interesting journey into the past with a fellow Manchester United player and captain born sixty-two years before me. I always said that one of the good things about working at the PFA was the sheer variety of matters that had to be dealt with in the course of my daily toil and Fergus's call was both unusual and compelling.

I won't spoil the story for you but Fergus and his group of dedicated colleagues were on a mission to raise funds for a fitting memorial for Patrick, who sadly was buried in an unmarked grave in 1959. I am delighted to have been able to help at our end by tracking down Patrick's PFA membership details in our crumbling ledgers of a century ago, and also by introducing our chief executive, Gordon Taylor, to a deputation including Mike and Sue O'Connell. Gordon was only too happy to pledge financial support for the project and I had the honour of being invited to Dublin to represent the PFA when a plaque was unveiled outside Patrick's childhood home. It was particularly pleasing to see former Celtic foes from my days at Aberdeen, now good friends, Bertie Auld and John Clarke at the ceremony.

There is an amazing list of world-famous footballing names who have made contributions or donations of memorabilia towards this great cause. Forgive me if I mention two: my hero, Franz Beckenbauer, who made the game look so simple and Sir Bobby Charlton, who did much to make me feel welcome when I joined Manchester United in 1972.

As I near the end of my own working career – well I am sixty-seven – Patrick O'Connell's story and the dedication and determination of his admirers will be one of my abiding memories.

Martin Buchan, PFA Executive

Martin started his career with Aberdeen FC, making his first team debut in October 1966 aged seventeen years and seven months and played as a centre-back for Manchester United between 1972 and 1983, captaining the team for six years. He was signed from Aberdeen by Manchester United in 1972 for £125,000, and was the club's record signing at the time. He led United back to the top division after the despair of relegation in the 1973/1974 campaign and captained the team to victory in the 1977 FA Cup Final against Liverpool. He left the club in the summer of 1983, having made 456 competitive appearances and scoring four goals. He won 34 caps for Scotland (captaining the side twice), and represented his country in the 1974 and 1978 World Cup finals. He is the only player to captain both Scottish and English FA Cup-winning sides (Aberdeen, 1970, and Manchester United, 1977). He joined the PFA as a full-time executive in 2000.

Martin Buchan, pictured right, with author, Sue, seated in wheelchair and her husband Mike, grandson of Patrick O'Connell, behind her.

The Patrick O'Connell Memorial Fund

It started as a chance meeting at Blyth Spartans FC where Fergus Dowd, Alan McLean and Simon Needham heard Mike O'Connell speak about his grandfather Patrick. They were very struck by the story of this amazing Irishman, Patrick O'Connell, who achieved so much in football. They decided to raise funds to put a headstone on his grave in London.

That was the start of an incredible journey to make Patrick's story known and it has been an absolute privilege for me to be part of that journey, with the Patrick O'Connell support group, especially Fergus and Alan, all committed to telling that story. My role in that journey began in January, 2015, when contacted by Fergus as I was TD (member of Parliament) for Dublin Central where Patrick lived. That first meeting led to many more meetings that culminated in a campaign to secure support through Dublin City Council to erect a plaque at the house on Fitzroy Avenue where Patrick lived. I was very honoured to be part of the unveiling of the plaque with Mike O'Connell and Martin Buchan. Then, with the support of the office of Dublin's Lord Mayor, we held a seminar evening and again it was an honour to chair the event in The Mansion House, Dublin, to honour Patrick. This was attended by many figures from the world of sport. That evening we had three trophies on show: Glasgow Celtic's European Cup, brought there by Celtic legends Bertie Auld and John Clarke who have become great friends of this project; the FAI Junior Cup, brought by Liffey Wanderers; and the Empire Cup which Patrick won three times as a teenager.

Through my engagement with Diplocat in Catalonia, contact was made with FC Barcelona, who were very keen to honour Patrick, the manager who saved the club during the Spanish Civil War. In late December we attended the match in Camp Nou between Barcelona and Real Betis, met the presidents of both clubs and presented Barcelona with a painting of Patrick who is the first Irishman to be honoured by the club.

The FAI will honour Patrick with an alcove in Abbotstown and Manchester United's museum will accept and display paintings of their four Irish captains, the first of whom was Patrick. Belfast has already honoured Patrick with a mural on the Falls Road.

Patrick had phenomenal success in sport but it's very sad that his personal life was fraught; he ended up homeless, his latter years in poverty, struggling with addiction and then buried in an unmarked grave. The constituency I represent, where Patrick lived, knows homelessness, poverty and addiction. Unfortunately, the inequality gap is widening. Those experiencing homelessness and addiction today would, like Patrick, have been successful in various walks of life.

I know that, for Sue, writing the book has been a labour of love. It has been an exciting journey for all of us and I feel very honoured to have been part of it with Fergus and Alan, with Mike and Sue and I acknowledge their passion and commitment to Patrick.

Ar dheis dé go raibh a anam dílis.
Maureen O'Sullivan
TD Dublin Central, Member of the Irish Parliament

Maureen O'Sullivan, pictured centre, with Bertie Auld and John Clark, both Lisbon Lions and supporters of the memorial fund in the Belfast Celtic museum where Patrick began his professional career.

Preface

Dan's Story
Dun Laoghaire, Ireland
March 1959

The Telegram

Your father died yesterday STOP Funeral Friday STOP Larry

*

On the quayside there was a flurry of activity. A woman hurried along with four young children. One of the children slipped. The woman helped the child to his feet.

The ship moved toward the open sea. A few passengers leaned over the deck rails, watching what was happening. One flourished a handkerchief and began waving with it, in an exaggerated fashion.

Dan walked along the deck to join the group of people, turning up the collar of his coat as he went. He thrust his hands back into his pockets. The telegram crackled between his fingers, small change caught in the folds of paper.

'Will you be travelling over for the work?' a man asked.

'No, I will not. A funeral. It's a funeral that I'm travelling over for.'

'A sad thing.'

'My father.'

The man crossed himself.

'May he rest in peace.'

'That's unlikely.'

The man hesitated for the briefest of moments, he then opened a pack of cigarettes and offered one to Dan.

'The grief of losing a father is a terrible thing.'

'Is it shite!' Dan said.

The man held out a light. He shielded the flame with his hands.

'A couple of dozen hours in my entire life, that's what I spent with him.'

'Why then are you going to the funeral, if that's the case?'

'Curiosity,' said Dan. 'That and my brother and my mother and my sisters will not be there.'

'Is that so?'

'What better reason to go to my father's funeral could there possibly be?'

The man looked carefully at his cigarette. The wind caught a flake of ash and carried it away.

'I'll be down to the bar, if you want to come and join me. A glass of whiskey is a great solace when you have a long journey and a sad arrival. When all is told, he was still your father.'

1908

'It's a remarkable thing,' said the foreman, pursing his lips. 'A truly remarkable thing that you are ill again and today a Saturday.'

Behind the man, Patrick could see a fellow worker doubled over in mock pain. Patrick ignored him.

'It's the dust,' he said. 'A week of breathing the flour dust and it has a terrible effect on the lungs.'

'It would seem,' continued the foreman, 'you have selected the wrong profession. You're not strong enough for this job.'

Patrick agreed.

'We'll see what happens a week from today.'

The invalid inclined his head slightly and turned towards the main door.

'Slow down, will you,' the fellow worker said under his breath, as Patrick passed by. 'At least, show that it costs you an effort to get out of here. You look the picture of health, walking at that pace.'

'By tomorrow,' Patrick said, 'this might well all be behind me.'

'The luck of the man,' said the worker. 'The luck of the man.' His words were lost as Patrick caught up his overcoat and football boots and was down the steps and out across the yard.

*

One of the players kicked the football up the pitch. The leather was absorbing more water by the minute. Patrick intercepted the ball and continued on with the attack. His toes were pinched and crushed but today he could ignore play without any discomfort. Today things were good.

He gasped for breath and passed the ball.

A cheer went up from the spectators.

The contract was there for the signing. It was his.

'Wake up, Patsy. Where are you at?'

Patrick darted up the pitch and tackled the winger.

The whistle went. The spectators went on cheering.

Fellow players surrounded Patrick. Some threw their arms around his shoulders. Others shook his hand.

'You'll be leaving us. On to Belfast Celtic and there will be no stopping you.'

A man in a suit stepped on to the pitch. 'That was a fine game you've just played. Join us in the Club Room. We'll be waiting for you.'

The other players surged forward and Patrick was carried along with them.

'Check no mud is showing. That's my dah's advice,' said one of the men. 'No mud showing and they'll know that you're a gentleman as well as a fine player.'

'Get in there and sign. The contract's yours. Go on now, will you?'

The man in a suit welcomed Patrick into the club house.

'There's a private room for us. A place where we might hear each other speak.'

He held the door open for the young player.

'That was a fine game you played today. We can all agree on that.'

Patrick nodded.

'You are twenty-one?' someone asked.

'Eighth of this month.'

'Good. Then we don't need anyone to sign on your behalf. You've attained your majority and, if you are in agreement, we will go ahead. The man tapped the page with his forefinger. 'Sign here, here and over the page.'

Patrick picked up the contract and read it.

'It's time to leave Liffey Wanderers behind and join a professional club.'

'It is.'

'We want you in Belfast by mid-August.'

Patrick dipped the pen in the inkwell and signed.

The assembled men took it in turn to shake his hand.

'You've a great future awaiting,' said one of them. 'See how things develop next season and you will be on the move again.'

Outside the ground, Patrick folded over the pages of the contract and put them in his coat pocket.

He jumped onto a tram on Sackville Street and made his way towards Drumcondra.

Turning into Shaid Maible, he saw his brother Larry, standing on the pavement in front of their house.

'Got it,' Patrick shouted. 'The contract. I've got it in my pocket. I've signed.'

'That's great.' said Larry. 'That's great but you'd better go without making so much noise, Father McQuirk is here.'

'And why is that, then?' asked Patrick.

'He's here to discuss the wedding.'

'And whose wedding would that be?'

'Yours,' said Larry. 'And could you see to lending me your boots for Wednesday?'

1909

**Ellen's Letter from Belfast
to Her Family in Dublin
March 1909**

Dear Everyone

This is a short letter to let you know that Patrick is playing football in Dublin next Saturday and I will be coming to see you all. Of course, this does mean that we will travel with all the crowds, but Patrick says we must take advantage of the excursion fares.

It is now certain that we are moving to Sheffield, as Patrick's new club is to be Sheffield Wednesday. We will have to be there by mid-August in order to give us time to settle in before the new season starts. At least that means we will be able to spend part of the summer with you all. Patrick has promised that we will stay there in Sheffield for two seasons or even three. It's too difficult to move every year, especially now we have baby Patrick. I can't help but wonder what it will be like to live there. This is a lovely city and sometimes feels just like home, but then there are times when I wish we were back with you all, especially as they never miss the opportunity to tell you what they don't like about you and that we are the ones who are out of place here. What will it be like to live surrounded by them on all sides? I don't always like to think!

You will be delighted when you see baby Patrick. You will scarcely recognise him at all. He grows day by day, he really does, and is getting so big now that I will need you to help me at the station.

Please be there to meet us as Patrick will have to go off straight away to get ready for the match and I do so find it difficult to manage on my own. We are due to arrive at 11:15 a.m. and will have the whole day together, as we don't have to return again until after 8:00 p.m.

I am looking forward so to seeing you and will wear my new hat for the occasion.

Your loving

Ellen.

Ellen's Letter from Belfast
to Her Family in Dublin
April 1909

Dear Everyone

What a delight it was to spend the day with you. Since our return however, there have been very sad events. The husband of one of our neighbours has been killed at the dockyards. So many of the men who work there sacrifice their health and their very lives in the construction of these ships. His widow is beside herself with grief and the poor woman now has the responsibility of raising four young children on her own, with scarcely any money to her name.

It is a great comfort to me that Patrick is employed elsewhere and does not have to risk his life as a matter of course. It would be a terrible grief to me to lose him. I cannot bear even to consider it.

Although the dockyards bring sorrow they also offer fascination. Only last Sunday Patrick and I took a walk with young Patrick in his new baby carriage. We went to get a glimpse of the liners that are under construction. We are told that the *Titanic* and its sister ship the *Olympic* will be the largest moving objects in the entire world. People are already saying that the launch of these two ships will be truly spectacular and that when fitted out, these liners will be the last word in luxury. It is of particular interest to Patrick to learn that when the *Titanic* is completed, it will be the length of three football pitches. It takes the breath away. It truly does.

Here life is very busy. Patrick is preparing for his move to Sheffield Wednesday and baby Patrick and I will soon be back with you in Dublin to stay for a while.

We send all our best wishes.

Your loving daughter,

Ellen.

What am I doing? I've forgotten to tell you the most important news. Baby Patrick has smiled. It was a beautiful moment and gave us both so much pleasure. He is aware of what is happening around him and spends a lot of time looking at Patrick and at me. I do believe he knows us already. He grows so quickly that I can scarcely keep up with the clothing he needs. Baby Patrick now has a perambulator. It is of the highest quality. Patrick has come round to thinking it was money well spent. He says it will serve our other children (when they arrive).

Ellen's letter from Sheffield
to Her Family in Dublin
August 1909

Dear Everyone

This letter is to let you all know that we have arrived safely and now I am able to send you our new address.

We have taken a small house, quite close to the football ground. Patrick is already training for the coming season and has been offered the opportunity to work as well. It is good that he was able to organise all this before we arrived.

Sheffield is such a busy place and I have to say that I prefer living here to living in Belfast, though I do so miss the sea. We will have to take Young Patrick to the seaside when I am next home with you to let him paddle and it will strengthen his ankles so.

Patrick has the offer of a job in a factory. This will help us out when the Team takes its summer break. The job has been arranged for him, organised by the team manager. The Managing Director where Patrick is going to work is said to be a great football supporter. I believe that he is also one of the men who founded the Club. This means that Patrick may take time out from his employment to get to the matches and also allows him to attend training. Patrick is very well thought of by the management and players alike.

I am delighted to tell you that Young Patrick is growing very well and strong. I am sure he will take after his father.

I'm awaiting your next letter.

Your loving,

Ellen.

1912

Ellen's Letter from Hull
to Her Family in Dublin
September 1912

Dear Everyone

As I write this letter, I am sitting by the open window, hoping to enjoy a breath of air. It is past 10 o'clock in the evening and the temperatures remain those of the hottest of summer days. Nor do these temperatures show signs of abating. Patrick is to be found on the front doorstep, talking to a neighbouring family and Young Patrick is asleep in the next room, covered only by the thinnest of cotton sheets.

In my present condition, with the baby due so soon, I am finding it so hard to do anything whatsoever and this heat serves only to make life difficult twice over.

On Saturday last however, I did manage to get to the football ground, to watch Patrick play. He was in excellent form and Hull City beat Glossop 2-0, in the main thanks to him.

One of the staff at the club fetched me a chair and so I was able to divide my time between watching Patrick play football and watching Young Patrick play with the other children. Thank goodness he no longer wants to be carried nor to use the baby carriage. It is such a great pity that Patrick is here so infrequently to help me and that the demands of the football season and of training take him away so often.

As the afternoon progressed at the football match, many of the gentlemen spectators removed their jackets and some even took off their waistcoats. Several players had to be carried off the pitch – overcome by the heat. Buckets of iced water were provided around the grounds, for everyone to refresh themselves. The weather does not seem like England to me, the country I read about in books, but like some faraway country or somewhere in the desert.

Before I close, there is something of great importance that I must tell you. There is to be a display with a flying machine. Patrick says that we must take Young Patrick to see this, as one doesn't know whether it will ever happen again. There is to be a race from Hull to Scunthorpe and back, all in one afternoon. What is more, it is rumoured that a lady aviator will take the controls for part of the flight. This causes great mirth in some quarters and surges of support in others. I am delighted to say, Patrick gives his support to the latter group.

I suspect that I can hear Patrick coming back in. I must close now.

We send our fondest wishes to everyone.

Your loving daughter,

Ellen, Patrick and Young Patrick.

PS. With a little persuasion Patrick has agreed that I will need an entire new wardrobe of clothes after the arrival of this next baby.

1913

Patrick's Letter from Hull
to His Brother Larry in Dublin
May 1913

Dear Larry

It appears that we will be off again to continental Europe. The organisation of the summer tour to Belgium is almost at the ready.

There's nothing like a change of scene after a long and tiring season.

The memory of the 11-1 victory over Trondheim, during last year's tour to Norway, remains fresh with the team. They look forward to new challenges and more victories such as this.

When are you coming over to England?

Your brother,

Patrick.

1914

Ellen's Letter from Hull
to Her Family in Dublin
May 1914

Dear Everyone

By the time this letter reaches you, we will have left Hull and have moved to Manchester so Patrick might take up his new job at United. Already Patrick has found us a house to rent and has written to tell me that it is in Collyhurst. Though as yet I know nothing of the city, I must wonder whether it is suitable for us all. The description Patrick has sent is a little vague. Sometimes I fear his choice is not what it might be.

It is with contrary feeling that I leave Hull. Patrick's football career develops very well and he is being transferred to Manchester United for the magnificent fee of £1,000. This reflects the esteem in which he is held. I believe it to be the second or third highest fee ever to be paid for a professional footballer.

We would be rich indeed if this fee were for us, but unfortunately this is not to be. Patrick is to be paid 10/- for his transfer and there is some dispute as to whether the Club will help with our removal expenses.

I am, of course, delighted that we are moving closer to you all. From Manchester it is only a short journey to the ferry and then to Dublin. It is my intention to get us all settled into the house in Collyhurst and then to travel home to be with you all by mid-July. Children as we know, decide when they are ready to be born. However, now that I have some experience in these matters it would help greatly if one or two of you came down to the North Wall to meet me.

Patrick will not be travelling with us, as he has to remain here in Manchester for training with the Club and also he must be available for the start of the new season. Young Patrick does try to care for me whenever possible, but Nancy still needs to be carried, which is increasingly difficult for me at this time.

When we leave Hull we will also leave Willy behind, which is a great sadness for us. His company is such a pleasure and he and Aida are so fond of the children. He tells me he is reputed to be one of the finest dentists in the entire city, though I do believe the tale grows in the telling. He promises to stop off in Manchester and visit us on every journey they make to Dublin. He tells me as though looking after him and his family is a delight for me to look forward to – the effrontery of the man. Yet then he says something that makes me laugh and all is forgiven. What a brother!

Patrick, Young Patrick, Nancy and I send our fondest wishes to you all.

Your loving daughter and sister,

Ellen.

Ellen's Letter from Dublin
to Her Husband Patrick in Manchester
August 1914

My Dear Patrick

This letter comes to you to let you know that we have another daughter. She was born on the 1st August and is a fine, beautiful child.

Your mother has been a wonderful support to me since the moment we all arrived. She has cared for the other two young ones, despite her advancing years and even now is helping me so that I might soon regain my health and strength.

Young Patrick is so pleased with his new sister and often asks when she will be able to come out to play with the other children. Everyone is delighted with this.

As soon as the child came into this world your mother exclaimed that she was another Ellen and so she had been baptised. People say that she resembles me in looks, as well as name.

It had always been my intension to return to Manchester in early October. There are however, terrible warnings and rumours that fly around this city. Everyone speaks of the submarine boats, which stalk all shipping between Dublin and England. With a word from the Kaiser, these ships will be sent to the bottom of the Irish Sea.

It would be a dreadful thing if your wife and children and new babe-in-arms were all to perish as they came back to you. When it is safe once more to cross the water, I will telegram to let you know of our arrival.

Your loving wife and children.

Ellen, Young Patrick,

Nancy and baby Ellen.

Although already she is being called 'Nell' and I think will remain so.

Many of the local men are interested in your progress and I am told that you scored the winning goal in your first match with Manchester United. We are very proud of you.

Ellen's Telegram from Dublin
To Her Husband Patrick in Manchester
October 1914

Patrick STOP Arrive Saturday STOP Ellen

Ellen's Telegram from Dublin
To Her Husband Patrick in Manchester
November 1914

Patrick STOP Were delayed STOP Arrive Tuesday STOP Ellen

Ellen's Telegram from Dublin
To Her Husband Patrick in Manchester
December 1914

Patrick STOP Will arrive Wednesday next STOP Ellen.

Ellen's Story
Manchester
December 1914

'What's this? I said, "What's this?" Patrick, Patrick I'm speaking to you. What is it?'

Patrick folded his newspaper and set it down on the table.

'Let me see now.'

He weighed the object in the palm of his hand and turned it this way and that.

'No idea,' he said.

'I'll tell you what it is. It's a hairpin. That's what it is. It's a hairpin.'

'There you are. The mystery is solved.'

He reached out for the newspaper.

'It's not my hairpin.'

'Isn't it, now?'

'No, it is not and I want to know what it was doing in my bed.'

'Our bed.'

'What it was doing in my bed.'

'You'll have picked it up by mistake. I don't know. It will belong to one of your sisters.'

'I haven't unpacked yet.'

'You will have picked it up by mistake. Your things will have got mixed with theirs. It's happened before. Heaven alone knows you were with them for long enough.'

'What's that supposed to mean?'

'It means exactly what I said. You stayed in Dublin for long enough.'

'And what did you expect me to do, Patrick? Patrick.'

He put the newspaper down again.

'Yes?'

'What did you expect me to do?'

'Come home.'

'I have had another child, in case you haven't noticed.'

'That was in August.'

'There have been submarine boats waiting to sink the ships. Did you wish us all to the bottom of the Irish Sea? Is that it? Patrick, I'm talking to you. Is that what you wanted?'

'Don't be ridiculous.'

'Don't talk to me like that.'

'Of course I didn't wish you to the bottom of the Irish Sea. It might have been better if you had come back to Manchester a little sooner. That's all I was saying.'

'You haven't answered my question.'

'What was that then?'

'Whose is it?'

'For the love of God. It's a hairpin. How am I supposed to know who it belongs to.'

'It's not my hairpin.'

'So you have said.'

'All I want to know is whose … now listen to what you have done.'

'Me? What I've done?'

'It took me an age to get the baby to sleep. Now she will be awake half the night and disturb the others.'

The windowpanes rattled as Patrick left the house.

Ellen stared at the door.

'How could you do this? How could you?'

Then she turned and went up the stairs. 'Hush now. Your Mammy is coming. Everything will be fine. Hush now.'

1915

Manchester Echo Football Edition
2 April 1915
By the Saturday Sportsman

As many of us left the grounds this afternoon we asked ourselves the question; what was the score, what was the true score of the match between Manchester United and Liverpool FC that was played this afternoon?

Manchester United FC v Liverpool FC
2   0

Was that the true score? A question mark must hang over it.

What a match it was. Catcalls and whistles, boos and jeers, right from the opening minutes. Half the players acted as though they would have preferred to be anywhere but on the pitch, playing anything but their chosen sport. One or two men behaved as though they had never before played a game of football in their lives.

This is not the sort of game the public has come to expect from these two teams, dare I say, these two illustrious teams. Over the years we have got used to performances of skill and energy, where men have been prepared to take risks. What we were treated to here were lacklustre displays, the like of which the public hasn't seen for a long time.

As for the penalty in the second half, it was indeed a strange penalty to watch. It made a mockery of this great sport. A dark cloud indeed hangs over that penalty. Every sportsman, every spectator must continue to ask;

'What happened at this match? What was going on?'

Keen supporters will argue that their team is coming to the end of a gruelling season. Many of the players are preparing to go and do their bit for King and Country. Others are already working in munitions helping to keep our fine lads at the Front well supplied with weaponry and armaments. No one will dispute this takes a toll on any man and everyman. Some will say these arguments go part way to explaining the mysteries of this match.

There are however, other supporters of these two generally great teams, who are starting to ask questions.

Was Liverpool FC in with a chance of relegation this season? Back comes the answer 'No, it was not.'

'Was Liverpool FC in with a chance of winning trophies and honours this season? Again back comes the answer 'No, it was not.'

What more can we say than that Liverpool FC was in a comfortable position in the League, nothing more, nothing less.

And was Manchester United in danger of relegation and the answer comes back, 'Yes, it was.'

It must be stated that the final score of 2-0 to Manchester United suited one team and did not do any damage to the other. It might in fact be said that it suited both teams admirably.

We can leave our readers to draw their own conclusions from this convenient result.

We can expect further questions to be asked. This reporter for one will not flinch from pursuing the true and correct answers.

The *Sports Reporter*
'The Football Kings'
Manchester
10 April 1915

It is not often that the great British Public is united together with the bookmakers and even less so when the event that links them, involves two football teams that are usually such arch rivals. Yet something has happened that conspires to bring about this very situation.

Flyers are already starting to be given out across the cities of Manchester and Liverpool and in many other places across the country. There is no doubt that these flyers have been printed with the backing of the bookmakers, the men who term themselves the Football Kings.

Many readers will recall the Good Friday Match of 2nd April 1915 between Manchester United and Liverpool FC, when we were given to understand that the result was 2v0, a win for Manchester United. This was a particularly fortuitous result given that Manchester United was in danger of relegation, whilst Liverpool FC was comfortably in the mid League table and could afford to be generous with regards to the outcome of the match.

Our readers will also recall that it was a match of dubious standards from beginning to end; questionable sportsmanship including a penalty shot which almost hit the corner post and a dispute between two players. The latter is more than common until we consider that the two players were from the same team and the dispute itself appeared to break out, not because the player had missed a goal but because he attempted to score it in the first place. This is not the game of football we know and have come to expect.

And what have the bookmakers to do with this? Up and down the country several of these men have been sharp enough to notice there was an unusual pattern outside the expected sphere of betting. There was a marked tendency for bets to be placed on the final score, a precise score of 2-0 on the match between Manchester United and Liverpool FC.

Moreover, several of these bets at odds of 7-1 no less, were placed by people who were recognised as being friends and family of certain members of the footballing fraternity.

Without doubt, bookies are willing to take bets on the outcome of a football match. Many spectators are ready to wage their hard earned cash on the possibility of their team winning the game. It is less likely though not unknown, for bets to be placed on the precise score of a match. Yet as far as this match was concerned, there was a marked preference for this pattern of betting. Was there more to this than mere chance?

Was it a remarkable coincidence or something more underhand that prompted men who lived as far away as Nottingham and Middlesbrough to wager large sums of money on the outcome of a match? We must ask why these men put their hard earned money on a final score of 2-0 in the Manchester United FC v Liverpool FC match of Good Friday 1915.

Was it merely an insight into the game after following the progress of the Teams throughout the season or was it something more? The whisper is going round that the game was squared and the final result was decided upon in a local hostelry several days before the match was played.

The public in general and football supporters in particular, have a right to expect a good, clean game and an honourable score as the final outcome. When working men decide to wager their money on the outcome of a match, that result must be due to the standard of play and its outcome, not to a decision made beforehand between players.

The conditions of honesty and fair play do not appear to have been met in this match.

A full enquiry is being demanded.

Patrick's Story
Manchester
April 1915

Always claimed that she had been there.

Ellen.

Always insisted that she had been at the match.

Told the children.

Told the family.

Always said that she had been at the match, that match on Good Friday.

But no, she wasn't there the day of the match.

She didn't come along that day.

She came along to other matches, certainly.

In the early days she often came along to watch the match.

But not that day.

That day she wasn't there.

All of them: Belfast Celtic, Sheffield Wednesday, Hull City, Manchester United.

Ellen came along. Brought the children too. Got more attention that way.

But that day she wasn't there.

You've got children and come along to the match?

'Hey, Missus. Is that your son? Is that your daughter?

And before you knew it Ellen would be there, telling them that she liked to bring the children along.

To watch their father. Their dah.

'One of the players?'

And Ellen would be modest and move her head a little to one side, the way she did, coquettishly and say:

'Yes. Yes, he is. The Centre Forward. He's my Patrick. The Captain.'

And people were impressed.

You could see it.

They were impressed.

And before you knew it, she would be in the stands, to get a better view.

She managed it every time.

On a good day she would end up in the Ladies Tea Room and someone would be looking after the children and offering to buy them lemonade.

Managed it to perfection.

But Ellen wasn't there, not that day.

She wasn't at the match that day, whatever she said.

Only Ellen could be selective with her memory, when it suited her 'Besides,' Ellen said 'It's Good Friday and I won't be coming to the match. The holiest day in the Calendar. No football. I won't be coming along.'
She could be religious in those days, sometimes.
When it suited her.

And it seemed it wasn't patriotic to go to football matches anymore. Not for the English.
Young men watching football, when they ought to be in the trenches or the munitions factories.
The muttering had begun.
The Great War. The War To End All Wars.
The War That Will Be Over By Christmas.
Only it wasn't over by Christmas.
Not that one. Nor the next one. Nor the one after that.
The young men.
They signed up in their droves.

And some of those that stopped behind asked:
Would football go on to the end of the season?
Would the League continue?
No one stopped the horse racing, now did they?
No. That was different.
The horse racing that was for the rich, the toffs and no one wanted to stop that, at all?
And the football struggled on to the end of the season
Easter 1915 and the writing was on the wall.
And Kitchener was pointing from his poster.
And the young men signed up and marched off.
And when they were home on leave.
What was it they needed?
Football. Enough to take their minds off things.
Forget the trenches for a day or two.
But some thought that a game of football was too good for them. The righteous bastards.
Soldiers on leave. Community hymn singing and nothing else to distract them from the next round of slaughter.
That's all that some people would have allowed the poor men, the poor soldier boys. Doing the bidding of their betters, the bidding of the very well-off-indeed. Doing their masters' bidding and dying for somebody else's will.

Fighting wars for others to make a fortune. Always the same. Poor suffer, the rich get richer.

Never did understand what they were fighting for.
Why were the lads were going to fight the Hun, after a couple of Royals had been assassinated in Sarajevo? Never did know.
Never did understand.
When they came back missing a leg or two or they'd left their minds and their souls in the trenches, the lads needed something to take their attention off things.
Or when they came out of the munitions factories after another interminable shift.
Football was too good for them.
Men wasting their time at football matches.
No distractions from the War Effort allowed.
And the lads who were still playing knew it was their turn next.
Their duty.
They knew it was for them to sign up as well.
The end of the season in 1915 was the end of the road, so to speak.
What would you do if you found yourself in that situation?
Answer me truthfully.
You'd feel it your duty to sign up, wouldn't you?
You'd know that your nearest and dearest were to be left with next to nothing.
And if this War ends and by some miracle you'd survived, you'd be too old to take up where you left off.
To return to the pitch and play like you used to.
And then the chance to earn a little extra comes your way.
I ask you this; 'What would you do?'
Tell the truth. Even the purest soul would have done the same as those lads.
If you were expected to risk all for your country, the least you could do is leave your family with a crust to keep them from starvation when you'd gone.
Don't tell me you wouldn't have done the same yourself.
And did I know or didn't I know?
Well now, I'll leave you to decide that for yourself.

And when they had their enquiry, down in London.
All those stuffed shirts sitting behind that polished desk.
All sitting in judgement, the least I could do was to get a laugh from them.
And perhaps they wouldn't be so hard on the lads who looked after their own.
But too harsh on those young men, they were.
And one of the lads even had to die to be forgiven.

Died in the trenches and then they received a posthumous pardon.

I ask you: What good would that do for them?

I ask you. You consider it.

Allow them to play in a Celestial Eleven?

But Ellen wasn't there that day.

By then she didn't come to the matches too often. Not like in the early days.

And my visit to London to the Football Enquiry, I met up with Larry and I got my self a job in munitions, down there I would still travel up to play for United, though it was terrible thing, working all week then travelling up to Manchester overnight on the railway train, playing a game and them back to London for another week of work.

Hard I grant you, though nothing to standing in the trenches and being shot at by other poor lads who didn't know what they were fighting for either.

I was young.

Things had changed.

Life was different.

I didn't blame the footballers at all.

Which one of you wouldn't have done the same, if you had found yourself in their situation? Answer me that.

1919

**Ellen's Letter from Manchester
to Her Family in Dublin
August 1919**

Dear Everyone

It might come as a surprise to you to learn that we are to move once again, after we have settled so well in Manchester.

You will no doubt recall my telling you of Patrick's playing in the Victory International held last March. These football matches were part of the festivities to celebrate the successful conclusion of the Great War. Patrick's playing was such that it was remarked upon and he has been offered the opportunity to play for the Scottish team of Dumbarton. Needless to say, he will be sorely missed by Manchester United, even though he won't be able to play for much longer. However, it seems this is an advantageous post and offers excellent opportunities.

The idea of moving is a little tiresome, especially now that Young Patrick and Nancy attend school. Yet, we are to understand that it gives Patrick the possibility of continuing with his playing career for a season or two. What is more, this time will prove useful for him to look for a post as a manager. So, move we must.

Young Patrick looks at his school atlas and tells us that Dumbarton is situated on the Clyde, a little North of Glasgow. Though the town is industrial, Loch Lomond is close by and is said to be very beautiful. We will have an opportunity to visit it, I trust. What is more Young Patrick informs us we will live quite close to the town of Stranraer and the ferry crossing to Ireland. All told there are many advantages to moving.

One of his fellow players has let it be known that there are manufacturing jobs available in the motor industry in the nearby area. Patrick will surely be able to find well-paid employment within days of our moving to Scotland, especially now that he has such experience in this trade.

Everything has happened so quickly I scarcely have time to take it all in – why it was almost organised before Patrick even mentioned the move to me.

Now I must return to my packing. Our lives are changing so quickly. As soon as we have our new address, I will write to you again.

Your loving daughter and sister.

Ellen, Patrick and the children.

Nell's Story
Recalling the Visit to Loch Lomond
September 1919

We went for a picnic and then we got lost. Only we didn't really get lost.

We all went on the picnic Mother and Patrick and Nancy and Dan and me.

I don't like Dan.

I do really but he's such a baby and he cries when he doesn't get what he wants.

We went on a picnic to Loch Lomond.

It was lovely.

We went by bus and we got lost when we came home, only we didn't really.

We surprised Father.

When we went on our picnic Patrick and Nancy sat together on the bus.

Nancy said Patrick kicked her.

He said she was lying.

He said he was practising a goal shot.

He wants to be a footballer like Father.

Father was Captain of Manchester United for a long time.

He's the best footballer in the whole world.

Mother looked at Patrick and Nancy with her stern look and they both kept quiet.

Mother said, 'One more word from either of you, Patrick and Nancy and you both go home.'

After that they were good.

I sat next to Mother

Dan sat on Mother's knee.

He fell asleep.

He missed the bus ride to Loch Lomond because he was asleep.

Lots of people got off the bus at the Loch.

Mother held my hand but sometimes she held Dan's hand when he walked.

Dan fell over and he started crying.

Mother gave the picnic basket to Patrick and Nancy to carry between them. And she picked Dan up and carried him.

Mother says that he's getting heavy. She says she won't be able to carry him much longer.

Mother carried Dan for a bit and then she put him down.

'What a hot day,' said Mother.

She fanned her face with a folded serviette.

'It's a grand day for a picnic. It is,' said Mother. 'It's a great pity your Father isn't here with us now to enjoy it'

And Patrick said it wasn't fair.

'Why can't Father be here with us today?'

And Mother said, 'He's training.'

We all knew that.

And Patrick didn't say anything. He just ran off.

He got to the Loch before the rest of us.

When we all got to the Loch, Patrick had taken off his boots and was paddling.

We sat down on a little hill.

Mother said she would be better able to see us from there, when we went to play.

Mother had brought a blanket and the picnic basket.

She spread the blanket out on the ground, so that we could all sit down when we had our picnic.

We went to paddle in the Loch.

'Tuck your dresses up in your knickers,' said Mother to Nancy and me.

We went to paddle where Patrick was.

We didn't go right by him because he was with the other big boys and they were all splashing and misbehaving.

I didn't want to get my dress wet and I didn't want to get my knickers wet either, so I moved away but Nancy didn't.

Mother called to us that Nancy and I had to stay with Dan, so I held one hand and Nancy held the other hand and Dan was in the middle.

And when we got to the Loch, Dan jumped in the water and then jumped out again.

He was very surprised that the Loch was so cold.

Dan wanted to go back to Mother but Nancy said, 'Don't be silly. You'll get used to it in a minute.'

I wish I'd said that but I didn't think to say it. Nancy is big. She will be eight years old next birthday.

We jumped up and down in the water until it wasn't cold anymore.

We jumped over the little waves.

There are little waves on the Loch like there are waves on the sea but they are not as big as the waves on the sea and they're not salty either like the sea is.

I've seen the sea when we go on holiday to Dublin, to stay with the Granny O'Connell. It's the Irish Sea. We travel over that when we go back to Ireland for our holidays.

Patrick and the other big boys came running along the beach. Patrick and the big boys splashed us and tried to make us fall over.

Dan started to cry again.

He wanted to go back to Mother.

My dress got a bit wet and my knickers got a bit wet and they stuck to my legs. It was hard to walk with my dress and my knickers sticking to my legs.

Dan kept on crying, so we said in a moment we'll go back to Mother and Nancy said, 'Dan, stop crying or I'll smack you.'

He didn't stop crying and I said, 'Please stop crying, Dan,' and he stopped crying.

We stayed in the water until our feet went blue and Mother called us to have our picnic.

Mother had set out all the food on the blanket, just like it was a table and she said we must eat nicely like we do at home. Only there were no knives and forks.

Then Mother sent us back to wash our hands.

'Look at your hands,' said Mother. 'Just look at them, now and bring Patrick with you when you come back.'

So we went back to wash our hands in the loch and I washed my hands so there wasn't any sand on my fingers and I helped Dan wash his hands too and Nancy smoothed her skirt down because Dominic St Patrick was there and she didn't want him to see her knickers, especially as they were wet.

Only Dominic St Patrick isn't his real name, it's Dominic Fitz Patrick but Nancy thinks it's fun to be in love with a saint.

Mother said, 'I'll be having a little nap, so go and play, all of you.'

I didn't go and play. I stayed sitting on the blanket. I wanted to make a daisy chain but I couldn't find any daisies. Perhaps daisies don't grow in Scotland like they grow in Ireland and England.

Mother sat still for a long time. She wasn't asleep. She was pretending. She kept opening her eyes and looking at the Loch, when she thought I wasn't noticing.

After a while I wanted to find some daisies. I went to look for some but not far away.

Our neighbour from just by where we live stopped to talk to Mother. 'Hello,' she said. 'Hello, Mrs O'Connell. It's a grand day for a picnic. What a pity Mr O'Connell couldn't be here to share it.'

And Mother said, 'Hello. It is a great day, indeed. And it is a pity that Mr O'Connell can't be here but his football training keeps him away.'

And our neighbour gave a sigh and said, 'It's a great pity indeed. These men and their football training and I'll be leaving you to enjoy your nap.'

And Mother said, 'Thank you,' very politely and closed her eyes again.

I looked for daisies all afternoon and I paddled as well.

Then it got late and everyone got ready to go home and I had to go and get Dan and Mother wanted to know why had I left him on his own.

Dan and I walked along the beach, to look for Nancy and for Patrick. I held Dan's hand.

We found Nancy. She was playing with Dominic St Patrick's sister. Nancy doesn't like Dominic St Patrick's sister but she likes Dominic St Patrick and that's why she plays with his sister.

I said, 'We've got to find Patrick because we're going home.'

And Dominic St Patrick's sister said she had to go home too.

Then Nancy came with Dan and me and we went to find Patrick.

Patrick was playing football with the other big boys.

He's the best player and all the boys want him to play in their team.

He practises with Father.

Nancy said, 'Mother wants you to come with us because we are going home.'

And one of the boys in Patrick's team said, 'Where's your dah then?'

And Patrick said, 'My dah's training for the next match.'

We all knew that.

And Patrick kicked the football very hard and said he was going and it wasn't any good any more.

When we got back to Mother, she said, 'About time, I was wondering where you all had gone to.'

Dan said he was tired and wanted to go to sleep, but Mother said that he could sleep when we all got on the bus and he said he was tired now, but Mother took his hand and made him walk.

When we got to the bus stop, there were a lot of people there. They were waiting to catch the bus back home.

Nancy said we would wait for ever and ever and ever.

A bus came along and Mother said, 'Here's our bus now,' and Patrick said, 'That bus isn't going to where we live in Dumbarton,' and Mother said, 'We are going home another way,' and she looked at him with her stern look and he kept quiet.

We got on the bus and Nancy waved to Dominic St Patrick's sister, who was still waiting at the bus stop. Only really she was waving to Dominic St Patrick but pretending she wasn't.

Dan sat on Mother's knee and I sat next to her and after a long time we couldn't see the Loch any more and so I put my head on Mother's arm and fell asleep.

'Will you look where we are,' said Mother and that made me wake up.

I looked and there was a palace. And I said, 'Look. A Russian palace.'

And Patrick said, 'How can it be a Russian palace? We're in Scotland.'

I said, 'I was only pretending.'

'It's a factory,' said Patrick. 'They make cars there and because it was the Great War they made munitions and sometimes because it was the Great War, the men and women who worked there have all turned yellow.'

'Don't be stupid,' said Nancy. 'Men and women can't turn yellow.'

'Stupid yourself,' said Patrick. 'Look at them. They are yellow because of what was in the weapons and munitions they made.'

And we looked and some of the people were all yellow on their faces and their hands.

Nancy started to swing her feet. She wanted to kick Patrick and then she can say it's Patrick's fault.

We stayed on the bus until we got to the place where all the buses stop and the bus drivers get off to have a rest before they do the same journey again but from the other way, so they can go back to where they started the bus journey.

It was a bit confusing as I didn't know why we had to come this way home but mother said we were getting off the bus and we would wait for a while before we caught the next one. Mother said I had to keep hold of Dan's hand, so I held his hand very tight, especially when the other buses came along the road. I didn't want him to get run over.

We found a bench by where the buses stop. We sat there for ages and ages and ages. Dan was bored and so was Nancy and my brother Patrick was as well. They all wanted to go home and so did I, but I didn't say. We all wanted to go home.

Then Patrick jumped up and shouted, 'There's Father. There's our dah.'

'Sit down will you and wait,' said Mother, but Patrick wasn't listening. He wanted to be the first to get to Father.

We all followed my brother Patrick. Nancy and Dan and me. All of us. Father was very surprised to see us.

'What are you doing here now?' he said

'We caught the wrong bus,' said Mother. My brother Patrick started to say something but he stopped when Mother gave him one of her stern looks.

'Where are your boots?' my brother Patrick asked Father.

Father said, 'I left them after training. At the club.'

'And which club was that, then?' Mother asked.

And Father said, 'Oh, the one here.'

And Mother said, 'All that extra training, all on your own. We didn't know there was club practice today unless there is another football club here in Dumbarton. We thought you played for the only club in the town.'

Father didn't answer. I think he was tired. My brother Patrick said he was happy to see Father.

'It's a pity that you had to go training today,' said Mother, 'You missed a lovely picnic.' Then my brother Patrick started to say something, but Mother gave him another one of her looks and he didn't say anything.

I think that Mother had forgotten what had happened. She didn't remember we were going home the other way and she passed Dan to Father so that she could have a rest.

'It would be a grand idea to have a cup of tea before we all go home,' he said.

So we went to have a cup of tea. Only we all had a glass of lemonade and Mother and Father had a cup of tea. I think Father was tired after his extra training.

We were all very happy to see Father and my brother Patrick said, 'Can we have a game of football when we get home.'

And Father said, 'Sure, that's a grand idea.'

And this time we caught the right bus back to our house.

Ellen's Letter from Manchester
to Her Family in Dublin
December 1919

Dear Everyone

Please resume sending letters to our old address in Manchester. It is a blessing that Larry continued to rent the house here in Manchester on our behalf, when we were away in Scotland.

The accommodation in Dumbarton was most unsuitable.

Your loving daughter and the children.

Ellen.

1920

**Letter from the Granny O'Connell in Dublin
to Her Daughter-in-Law Ellen in Manchester
November 1920**

Dearest Ellen

You must not worry. Your son Young Patrick is here. He is here with me and he is safe from all the troubles and trials we are suffering in Dublin.

He came to Ireland by ship. Do not ask me how. I think he hid on the ship and got here unseen. He is safe, so do not worry. It did not cost him any money to travel like this.

Young Patrick came here looking for his father. I do not know where his father is staying right now. He might be with his brother Larry in London but he is not here. I would tell you if he was staying here with me or in Dublin at all.

As is right for a boy of his years, Young Patrick is interested in the sports here in Dublin. It is tomorrow I think when he will go to Croke Park. It is possible to see the Park almost from the road where we live now. It is a blessing to know he is so close by to his home here in Ireland in this time of trouble.

I will send your son Patrick back to you by Christmas. He is concerned about coming back to Manchester, as he did not ask your permission to come over to Ireland. I have told him he must write to you to explain his behaviour. I believe it is that he wants to see his father.

I will not send him yet, as it is a great pleasure to have him stay with me.

God bless you and the Children.

Your Mother-in-law O'Connell.

Young Patrick's Story
Croke Park, Dublin
November 1920

Young Patrick watched as the blood dripped over the edge of the step and seeped across the concrete floor towards where he stood. He willed himself to move away from the spreading pool but his legs wouldn't do what he wanted.

'Will someone get the child out and away from this.'

An old man began pulling him along by the arm. He moaned to himself as he dragged Young Patrick towards the exit.

'In the name of God, what have they done now? What have they done? God help us all.'

The old man stopped.

'Wipe your feet.' he said 'You've got blood on your boots. Your Mammy won't be wanting to see that.'

Young Patrick tried to tell him that he wasn't going home to his Mammy. He was going to the Granny O'Connell's house along the road but when he opened his mouth, no sounds came out. The old man gave Patrick a push in the direction of the gates. 'Go on.' he said 'Get yourself home and don't be staying around here. Get away out of here now.' There were huddles of people standing on the pitch. Young Patrick looked around. A priest was giving the Last Rites. The body was stretched out on the pitch.

A huddle of people stood around it. A woman was wailing and clutching at her shawl. The smell of rifle shot hung in the air.

A line of soldiers barred the entrance to Croke Park. They stood with bayonets fixed. Patrick skirted past them and made for the perimeter fence. There was a gap in the paling, where the local boys got in without the inconvenience of an entry charge. Young Patrick stopped. A boy of nine or ten years of age was blocking the gap.

'My dah.' said the boy, rocking backwards and forwards on his heels, 'My dah.'

He appeared not to notice Patrick.

'My dah.' he said again and was violently sick. A trail of vomit dripped down his jacket.

Young Patrick moved the boy to one side and then clambered through the hole in the fence. Crowds of people were surging around. It was just as it had been earlier; some people trying to get away from the ground, others to get in to it.

'Have you seen my son?' a woman asked. She caught at the sleeves of people, who passed by, 'Have you seen my son?'

'How were they to know?' Young Patrick thought, 'There had been thousands of people in the ground. How were they to know who was the woman's son?'

He stopped to pick up a handful of grass. He hadn't to let Granny O'Connell see him with blood on his boots. The man had told him that. As he tugged up the grass to wipe his fingers on, he caught sight of his hands. He stretched them out in front of him to examine them.

'You've had the rheumatic fever.' his mother had said. 'Wear your gloves. I don't want you getting ill again. Cheaper to buy a pair of gloves than to have to be paying for the doctor to visit.'

And Young Patrick had paid attention. He had worn his gloves as the ship sailed along the Manchester Ship Canal and across the Irish Sea and all the way to Ireland, yet somehow he had lost those gloves. He looked at his hands again to make sure he didn't have them on, he then turned and hurried back to Croke Park. Ahead of him, Young Patrick could see the woman still catching at the arms of everyone she passed 'Have you seen my son?' she asked again and again. 'Have you seen him?'

At the main entrance to the ground, a crowd had gathered. Young Patrick ducked down and wove between their legs. He stopped at the line of soldiers and considered his options.

'Here. You.' Young Patrick looked up.

'Yes, you. I'm speaking to you. Where do you think you're going?'

The soldier took a step towards Young Patrick. Young Patrick took a step back.

'I'm.' he said, 'I'm. I'm. My gloves. My Ma'll kill me if I lose my gloves.'

'And I'll kill you, if you go back in there.' said the soldier 'So, which is it going to be?'

Behind Young Patrick, a man began cursing the soldier. The boy turned and darted off through the crowd.

'Clear off, sonny' shouted the soldier, 'This isn't a place for you.' He continued to watch until he lost sight of the child.

'What's going on?' said the soldier to himself. 'That lad sounds English or almost English. What the bloody hell is he doing here? And going in there for a pair of gloves. What does he think he's on about?'

Letter from the Granny O'Connell in Dublin
to Her Daughter-in-Law Ellen in Manchester
December 1920

Dearest Ellen

It is a time of great strife and difficulties for us all here in Dublin and through all of Ireland. You will have learned of the terrible news of what is happening in this city and what has been done at the Park to the poor souls watching a sporting football match there.

The Park is close by. We could hear the sound of gunshots and we could smell the cordite in the air. We do not deserve this suffering. Your son is safe and has not been injured.

Young Patrick will come back to you by Christmas. It is as I said to you before. Yet he tells me he is troubled to come home to you as he left without your permission, to come here to Dublin to look for his father.

May God bless you and the children.

Your Mother-in-Law O'Connell.

1922

'The move from Dumbarton wasn't easy,' said Patrick.

'It wasn't easy for either of us or for the children. They want to see you,' said Ellen.

'Is that so? Danny seems quite content.'

He looked at the child for a moment.

'This move has given me the opportunity to work as a manager. You know I can't see a life for me outside football. It means a great deal.'

'More than your family?'

'I didn't say that. Football is all I've ever wanted to do and I do it well.'

'At the moment?' said Ellen. 'Do you play for the team or do you manage the team?'

'Both. I do both. Didn't you hear what I was saying just now,' said Patrick. 'I manage the team and when needed, I play.'

Patrick and Ellen each held one of Danny's hands. They lifted him high into the air and helped him land gently at the foot of the steps.

'Well done, Danny,' said his father. 'That was a grand jump that you've made.'

The child said nothing.

'Come on, Danny,' said his father. 'Are you not speaking to me now?'

'Leave him,' said Ellen. 'He's tired. We had to get up before five o'clock this morning, to catch the train.'

'Then he'll sleep on the way back,' said Patrick. 'He'll be no trouble.'

'I imagine,' said Ellen. 'And the others wanted to come as well. To see you, that is. They all wanted to come along.'

'Why didn't you bring them then?' asked Patrick.

'Travel with four children and on my own,' said Ellen, 'and besides I couldn't afford the fares.'

'I send you money. Every month.'

'I wasn't saying that you didn't but the girls need new winter coats. They're growing so fast. Both of them and have you any idea how much a decent wool coat costs?'

'I send you money,' said Patrick. 'Every month, without fail.'

'I'm not having my children do without winter coats,' said Ellen, 'not even if I have to do without food myself.'

'There's never been a question of that,' said Patrick, 'Never.'

They walked on in silence.

'How much did it cost to get a ticket for Danny?' asked Patrick.

'Nothing,' Ellen said. 'I told the ticket clerk that he wasn't four years old yet.'

'Is he not?' asked Patrick.

'You don't know how old your own son is?' said Ellen. 'He was five last March, if it is that you can't remember.'

'It's just that he's small for his age,' said Patrick. 'He takes after your family.'

Ellen turned to the child. 'Don't do that,' she said. 'It isn't nice and you'll ruin your shoes.' She tugged at the child's arm. 'And where do you think I'm going to get the money from to buy you another pair?'

'I'm not certain my contract is going to be renewed,' said Patrick.

'And?'

'Well, that's what I am telling you,' said Patrick: 'There are strikes at the pits.'

'What's that got to do with it?'

'Everything. If the miners are on strike, then they don't have the money to come to the matches, the takings are down and contracts – mine for one – won't be renewed.'

'You're not a player now, are you?' said Ellen.

'You didn't listen to what I was saying just now. I still play from time to time, but I train the team as well. That's my main work, training. I'm the manager as well as a player. No matches and the team doesn't need to be trained. It's straightforward. Since I moved from Dumbarton to Ashington I have become a manager. This experience with Ashington in an English league, could set me up for a future career as a manager.'

'And what are we meant to do?' said Ellen. 'What about the children? We can't live on fresh air.'

'I don't want to dispute in front of the child,' said Patrick. 'The refreshment rooms are open. A cup of tea would be good for us both.'

Patrick held out his hand to his son. 'Come on, Danny. Would you like a cake? Let's see what we can get for you.'

The waitress set down a plate in front of the child.

'There,' she said, 'a slice with a cherry on top for the little boy. Will there be anything else?'

'It's not easy finding another job,' said Patrick. 'I can't play football for ever, can I now?'

'Do you think it's easy for me?' said Ellen. 'On my own in Manchester, with four children and my mother in Dublin and your mother there too and you here?'

'Yes?' said Patrick. 'Better to wait until I know about my contract. Then we can think about you moving house.'

'It's no problem,' said Ellen. 'It would save all that expense.'

'I can't hear what you are saying,' said Patrick. 'Above the noise of the trains.'

'Nothing of importance,' said Ellen.

'Will you look at that,' said Patrick, 'the evening newspapers are arriving. Come on Danny. Let's buy a newspaper for your mammy. It will lighten the journey.'

He held out his hand to the child. Danny put the last piece of cake into his mouth and jumped down from his seat.

'We'll not be a moment,' said Patrick.

Ellen stirred her cup of tea.

'My dear,' said a woman at the next table. 'I think your husband is waiting for you at the door.'

'I hadn't noticed,' said Ellen.

Danny was pressing his face to the window of the tearoom.

'I want to go home,' he said.

Ellen took the newspaper that Patrick offered.

'There's a new cinema film with Chaplin. You'll enjoy that. It will be showing in Manchester next week. He's always so funny, that little man.'

He checked his watch again. 'We'd better go on to the platform. We don't want the train to leave without you, do we?'

Patrick and the child went through the ticket barrier.

'All the same, you ladies,' the ticket inspector said. 'Put something in a safe place and you can never find it again. Just like my wife.'

He glanced at the ticket.

'Coach E,' he said.

Ellen made her way between the other passengers.

'I prefer to face the engine,' she said.

'I'll do what I can,' said Patrick. He picked up the child and lifted him into the train. 'Here's a three penny bit for you. Ask your mother if she'll let you buy some sweets when you get back to Manchester.'

'What about the others?' said Ellen, 'Don't they get anything?'

Patrick dipped his hand into his jacket pocket again. He held out a shilling coin to the child. 'For Patrick, Nancy and Nell. Some sweets for them, too.'

Ellen took the coin. 'He'll only go losing it,' she said. 'I'll keep it for him.'

There was the sound of slamming carriage doors. A whistle blew.

'There you go, Danny,' Patrick said. 'A train ride all the way to Manchester and don't forget to count the stations on the way and let me know how many there are.'

'How can he do that?' said Ellen. 'He's only just learning to count and besides with you here and us in Manchester, how is he to tell you the answer? He can't write you a letter. He's too young.'

Patrick patted Ellen's hand and stepped back from the carriage. The train jolted and moved forward.

'Tell the others that their dah expects them to behave,' he said, then lifted his hat to wave the train out of the station.

'It would be no trouble to move,' called Ellen, leaning out of the carriage window, 'None at all.'

Patrick's Story
Ashington
May 1922

'A fine leather suitcase,' his mother had said so many times. 'A fine leather suitcase, so that you can hold your head up high as you set out into the world.'

'Indeed,' thought Patrick, 'it must have been his mother who had bought the suitcase for him and where she had got the money from to buy it, he didn't know. No doubt paying off a backstreet Dublin moneylender even yet.

Certainly, it must have been his mother who bought the case for him as he prepared for his first professional move – when he left Dublin for Belfast, the first move he and Ellen had made together.

The case must have been the height of quality as far as his mother was concerned, appropriate to meeting the supposed standards of his new wife's family. Patrick shifted the suitcase to his other hand. It had worn better than the marriage. It was still holding together and there was a polish on it. The handle was frayed but nothing a few stitches wouldn't sort and the metal clasps made a good, solid sound when snapped into place.

He could see the station and stopped again. A dull ache was spreading up his arm. It had never been right since that break he had had. Mind, the injury had been in a good cause and he had returned to the pitch in time for the Irish to hold the Scots to a respectable draw. The match with nine and a half men as the newspapers had proclaimed, one man sent off and him with his broken arm, as the half player. This was the team that had won the team the Home Championship of the 1913/14 season. The injury was in a good cause. His arm had never been quite the same though.

He walked on to the platform. One or two fellow passengers acknowledged him.

'Leaving us, Mr O'Connell?'

'I am.'

'Back to Ireland?'

'Not at present. No.'

'With the miners out on strike there isn't much going on here. Difficult when you've not got spectators.'

'It is. That it is.'

The man nodded and Patrick continued along to the ticket office.

He looked down the platform. All those respectable men, going to their respectable jobs. All those respectable women setting out for a day of shopping in Newcastle. And he was leaving all this behind. All those respectable people and their lives and the damp and the coal dust and the miners and their problems and he was leaving it all behind.

'Destination?'

'London.'

'Return?' the booking clerk asked.

'Single,' Patrick replied.

He counted out the amount and pushed it through the grill.

'Sir?'

Patrick's attention was drawn to the money lying on the metal tray. He took another coin out of his jacket pocket.

'Moving on?' said the ticket clerk.

'I am.'

They both looked at the train ticket.

'London. I've always wanted to go to London,' said the booking clerk.

'I've a brother who lives there.'

'Never been to London, myself.'

'You're young. Plenty of time yet. You'll get there. Good luck to you.'

Patrick picked up the suitcase again. He thought of the letter, folded in one of his football boots, that letter of invitation for him to join a football club in Spain. A week or so with Larry to give him time to deal with details of passports and visas and then ...

'The train approaching ...' The voice of the station guard could be heard above the hiss of the engine. The train halted in a cloud of steam.

Carriage doors swung open. Patrick walked along the southbound platform looking into the compartments until he found an empty seat. He swung his case into the carriage and then followed himself. 'If only they knew how southbound I am,' he thought. 'If only they knew.'

Patrick's Letter from Santander, Spain
to His Brother Larry in London
October 1922

Pension Niza

c/o Joaquin Costa

Santander

Spain

Dear Larry

Finally, I've arrived here in Spain, in Santander and isn't it the greatest place to be that I'm living – a goal shot away from the beach and the waves crashing on the sands.

The ship brought me into the harbour, green hills on either side of the approach to the port. At the water's edge were sheds for fishing boats and on the jetties sat women mending the nets. This is not the land of relentless heat I had expected. All told it puts me in mind of Ireland.

There was a welcoming committee to meet me (two men and a dog) and before I knew it, my passport was stamped and I was the country's most recent immigrant and labourer. Then I was away by tram along the strand to my new home – a walk away from the stadium. Shortly, it was off to meet the team and together aren't we going to do the greatest of things.

It's a marvel to me that the very language I need to do the job of manager is the language I have already: 'corner', 'penalty', 'off-side', not because the previous manager – a certain Mr Pentland, was English – but because this is the language used in Spain for the game of football. It is said the English sailors brought the game to the country and the language they used has remained. It is however, my intension to acquire the Spanish tongue, as otherwise my conversations will be limited in the extreme.

The Director of the Racing Club of Santander is a highly motivated, highly educated man who speaks English, though to manage the team with any degree of success I will have to use more than the ten words of English the men already understand.

Write to me here at the Pension Niza, my boarding house by the sea, my residence in Santander.

Your brother,

Patrick.

PS And what is between my new home and the sands? A casino. A majestic building with two flights of steps leading up to the entrance, two imposing domes and a terrace where the local grandees take a glass as the sun goes down. I'm told it's the greatest building of its kind this side of Montecarlo.

Patrick's Letter from Santander
to His Wife Ellen in Manchester
November 1922

My Dear Ellen

I trust this letter finds both you and the children in the best of health.

I enclose some Spanish pesetas, the most I can manage at present, as I have my own living expenses to deal with as well.

Take this money to Cook's. You will know his sports shop, where I used to buy my football boots. He will organise for these pesetas to be exchanged into English Pounds Stirling. He has family, his brother I believe, living abroad and is accustomed to these transactions.

I send no address, as my lodgings are temporary. I will write again in due course.

Tell the children I expect them to behave for their mother.

Patrick.

Spain is not as oppressively hot as I had imagined, though I am told it is so in the south of the country.

1924

When we were a proper family, I used to like Christmas time but now I don't. It makes me think of Father. Though I keep wanting to see him again, it makes me a little bit sad to remember him.

We used to live in Scotland at Dumbarton, with Father. He went there to play football but when we came back to Manchester, Father didn't come with us. It was nearly Christmas and there were carol singers in the street. Father came to the railway station to see us off. He told us to be good for Mother. When the train left the station Father waved to us and we waved to him. Only Patrick didn't wave. He sat in his seat, breathing on the windowpane of the carriage and drawing patterns in the mist with his finger. Mother was busy with Dan. He was trying to climb on her knee and wave to father at the same time. If she had noticed what Patrick was doing, she would have been vexed and have told him off.

Patrick told me he hates Father and is never going to speak to him again, though he is careful never to say that when Mother is listening. I told him it is wrong to hate anyone.

It was a long journey back to Manchester. Mother said, 'It's a blessing your Uncle Larry paid the rent for us when we went to visit your Father in Scotland.' This was a bit confusing as I thought we had gone to Scotland to live with Father. Mother says that footballers move so often because of their work. They have to move to the next team that offers them a good job. We have to wait in our house in Manchester until Father is settled with a new team. Then he will send for us.

When we got back to Manchester, we didn't have to sit on the pavement while Mother looked for another house for us to live in. Instead, we went back to our old house Uncle Larry had kept for us. Now we have our old bedrooms back again. I like that but I still miss Father.

Our first Christmas back in Manchester was not a happy time. We didn't get any presents and we didn't even have a proper Christmas dinner. Mother kept saying we ought to be grateful we had a roof over our heads. I think she meant it was good that Uncle Larry had paid the rent and we still had our house in Church Street to come back to.

Patrick says that fathers ought to be with their children, especially at Christmas time. I've said we will all be happy to see Father again, even if it's not Christmas.

After a few days when it was New Year, Mother told us we were going to stay in Manchester until we got a letter from Father, telling us where we were going to move to next. It's difficult being a footballer because the players have to move to where there are places in the team for them to play. Now he is a manager he has to wait until the new team needs him. I hope Father gets another job soon, so we will be able to go and join him. As he is the best footballer and the best manager in the whole world, I don't suppose we will have to wait very long.

Everyday when the postman comes along the street delivering letters, Dan and I wait by the front door in case one of the letters is for us. We have waited a long time but we haven't got a letter yet. We all feel miserable.

Because we were all unhappy Dan went into the back alley and collected some cats, lots and lots of them. He brought them home to make us happy, whole arms full of them, but the cats all ran away and we got sad again.

This story is what I remember. It is for my diary and no one else is to read it.

1925

Nell and Dan's Story
Manchester
October 1925

'Go on,' shouted the postman. 'Clear off, the lot of you.'

He readjusted his postbag and then lifted the bundle of letters to read the next address for delivery. The children held back a moment, before swarming around him once more.

'I don't want to have to tell you lot again.'

Two or three of the boys ran on ahead. Some of the girls dropped behind and sat down on a front door step.

'It's for Nell's mam,' one of them said.

'How d'you know?' asked her friend.

'Because, because who else gets letters from other countries round here.'

An upstairs window rattled open.

'Get off the steps,' a woman called. 'I whitened them not half an hour ago and I don't want you messing them up.'

The eldest girl jumped to her feet.

'My mam'll kill me if I get any whitening on my dress,' she said. 'Let's go and look for Nell.'

'Bet Dan's with her, as usual,' one of the other girls said.

They muddled along the street and stopped at the corner. The postman continued his delivery round.

'Why does Nell's mam get letters from other countries?' asked one of the girls.

'Because their dad sends them, that's why.'

'Why does he do that?'

'Because he's run off, stupid,' said her sister.

'Why did he do that?'

One of the other girls took it upon herself to enlighten the child in the ways of the adult world.

'Then they'll go to Mr Cooke's.'

'Why do they do that?'

'Why? Why? Why? Can't you say anything else?' asked the oldest girl. 'Nell and Dan go to change the money, that's why.'

'Why?'

'Because you can't spend Spanish money in Manchester, that's why and don't go on.'

The group of girls contemplated this for a moment.

The eldest girl realised she was losing her role as purveyor of information and resumed the explanation unasked.

'Mr Cooke used to be a footballer like Nell and Dan's dad. He's got a shop now and he keeps all his profits in a bank and Nell and Dan's mam, well she's a mam and doesn't do things like go to banks.'

'She borrows money from the ...'

'Shut up,' her sister said and gave her a sharp push.

'So she sends Nell and Dan to Mr Cooke's shop because he goes and takes the money to the bank and he knows how to change Spanish money into English money. Like they do in banks.'

The girls considered this explanation of the financial transactions for the O'Connell household.

'My mam says at least she can hold her head up.'

The older members of the group giggled at this.

'Look who's coming,' she said.

Nell walked past, with Dan at her side.

'Want to play?' one of the girls asked. 'Dan can come too, if he wants.'

'Thank you,' Nell said, 'but we are going home for our dinner.'

Behind her back one of the girls mimicked Nell's words. The girl caught sight of Dan watching her and stopped in mid-sentence.

'There's a letter for you,' the eldest girl called. 'It's foreign.' Then she tossed her skirt and lifted her arms in what she believed was a flamenco dance.

'I hate girls,' Dan said. 'Not you though, Nell. Race you home.'

And he and Nell took off running down the street.

They arrived at the house at the same time as the postman.

'I've got a letter for your mother.'

'She's busy,' Nell said. 'You can give it to us.'

'Not going to knock on the door, then?' the postman asked.

'We use the back gate,' said Nell. 'We go down the alley and use the back gate.'

'Tell your mother that I'm waiting here to give her this letter. It might be important.'

'We'll take it,' Dan said.

'He won't give it to us,' said Nell. 'Come on.'

The postman turned the envelope over once or twice, then examined the stamps. He heard footsteps in the hall.

'Who's that?' a woman called.

'It's the postman. I've got a letter for you.'

'Put it through the letter box, then,' she called back.

'It's a foreign letter. From another country,' the postman continued, 'It might be important.'

'A moment.' There was the sound of bolts pulled back. The door swung open.

'I'll take it,' said Ellen, as she dried her hands on her apron.

'I had to check. It's not often that people around here get letters like this, not from foreign parts.'

'No,' said Ellen. 'No, I don't suppose they do.' She held out her hand for the envelope. The postman gave it a final glance before handing it over.

'My lad would love those stamps,' he said. 'That is, when you've finished with them.'

'I'm sure,' she said and closed the door.

In the dark of the hallway, Ellen paused for a moment and pressed the envelope between her fingertips, then dropped it into her apron pocket.

The two children were standing in the doorway to the kitchen.

'What is it that you are wanting now?'

'You told us to be back by twelve o'clock,' said Nell.

'Did I now? I suppose I must have done. I've a message for you to do, after you've eaten your dinner.'

'Can we buy some ...' Dan said.

'What was that?' Ellen asked.

'Some sweets,' the child said.

'Didn't I say, now?' said Ellen. 'A penny each for you.'

'First to Mr Cooke's and then to the corner shop.'

'They won't serve us anymore at the corner shop,' said Nell. 'We owe 7/6. Since the summer.'

'There'll be no problem after you've been to Mr Cooke's and changed this in to English money. Then you can call at the corner shop and give them five shillings. Five shillings at the corner shop and no more, mind. They can wait for the rest. The people that have the shops don't do without.'

'That's what we told them last time. At the corner shop,' said Nell. 'We only had five shillings.'

'Yes,' Ellen said. 'and that's what you can tell them this time, as well.'

The children trooped into the kitchen after their mother.

'When I'm big,' said Dan, 'I'm going to have lots and lots of money and eat hundreds and hundreds of sherbet dabs and caramel chews and never ever eat bread and marge and I'm going to drink wine with every meal.'

'Even with your breakfast?' asked his sister.

'I might because I'm going to have lots and lots of money and nobody will stop me. I'll do whatever I want.'

At two o'clock precisely Mr Cooke opened the shop for the afternoon's trade.

'How much have you got this time?' he asked of the two children.

Nell went over to the counter and put down a small wad of notes. Dan trailed behind her and stopped to examine some sports clothes.

'How's your football, Dan?' Mr Cooke asked, leaning over the counter. Dan went to join his sister.

'What's the matter then? Cat got your tongue?' The man offered two liquorice twists to the children. Nell stepped forward.

'Thank you,' she said. 'Thank you, Mr Cooke.' She gave Dan a gentle push. Dan in turn stepped up to the counter and took the other liquorice.

'Thank you. It's my favourite. I'll keep it for later,' he said.

1926

Ellie O'Callaghan's Story
London
April 1926

'There, now. There,' said the aunt, sinking into the chair. 'What bliss. It was worth the wearing of them, for the pleasure of taking them off.'

She leaned forward and gently massaged her toes.

'It would have been better to wear the other pair,' said Ellie.

'Good shoes. Good family,' said the aunt. 'I was not having you and I going into the Ritz Hotel, the Ritz Hotel in London and people thinking that we were not from the best of families.'

'I'd been in the Ritz Hotel before,' said Ellie. 'With Mrs Ashmede-Bartlett. I know what it's like. I've seen it.'

'The carpets,' said the aunt, 'I could scarcely bring myself to walk on them. A yard of that carpet must have cost a full year's wages.'

'The wages of people like us, but that's how the rich live. All the time. They don't even notice the carpets. They only notice when things aren't going right for the likes of them.'

She took a letter out of its envelope, unfolded it and read it with great care.

The aunt regarded her own stocking feet. She wriggled her toes.

'Keep that letter safe. You'll be needing it, when it's time to move on.'

'Aunt,' said Ellie. 'It's only today that I've got my new post. I'm a nurse to the children. The Mercer children. I can't be thinking of moving on just yet.'

'In my day,' began the aunt, 'it was getting someone to pay your passage over to England and never being out of work.'

'I know,' said Ellie, 'but the Mercers will be taking me. I'm going to France with them.'

'Your passage over to England,' continued the aunt. She disregarded Ellie's comment. 'And as soon as that was done, you had to work to pay the passage of the next brother, the next sister, who was to come over.'

'France,' said Ellie. 'It takes my breath away, though I'll be sending money home as soon as I get my first wages.'

'Is that right?' said the aunt. 'You had to get to work to pay the passage of the next brother, the next sister, as someone had paid your passage over.'

'By all their hard work and savings,' Ellie said under her breath.

'By all their hard work and saving,' said her aunt. 'Not by going off to France, with an English diplomatic family.'

'It'll be that I've more money to send to the Mammy,' Ellie said, 'from the very first time I get paid.' She put the letter away into its envelope. 'Thank you, Aunt. Thank you. Thank you. I couldn't have done this without you. The nerves I had this morning.' She kissed her aunt on the cheek. 'I couldn't have done this without your help and now I'm going to France.'

The aunt regarded Ellie. 'The dress becomes you,' she said. 'Now that it is a decent length.'

Ellie looked at her reflection in the hall mirror and lifted the skirt a little.

'I wasn't having a niece of mine walking along Piccadilly in a dress any shorter than that dress is now and what would I be saying to your mammy, if you did?'

'It was two o'clock in the afternoon,' said Ellie.

'The stories I've heard are not fit to be repeated,' said the aunt.

'Aunt.'

'In front of a young woman from a decent family.'

Ellie let go of the material and the skirt dropped back to its original length.

'I was wondering what the fashions are like in France.'

'Expensive,' said the aunt.

'I was wondering if everyone in France is fashionable.'

'The rich will be,' said the aunt. 'They always are. In Paris, in London, in Dublin.'

'It's just that I can't be wearing the uniform, the nanny's uniform, all the time, even on my day off.'

'The sin of vanity,' said the aunt.

'It's that I've heard that everyone in France is so fashionable.'

'Get something that wears well,' said the aunt. 'I recommend it.'

'But in France,' said Ellie.

'You'll be wanting to change for dinner next. And have the rest of us doing the same. Well, good luck to you. You've a life ahead of you. Now go along to the kitchen, will you? And cut us a slice of that lovely rich fruitcake, so that we can celebrate your future with that. There's more than a drop of brandy in it.'

Ellie's Letter from London
to Her Sister Mary in Ireland
May 1926

Dear Mary

It was good to hear from you, indeed it was.

Now you know I've written many letters to you all at home, but I have to say that you are the only one who replies to me. Isn't that strange? After thinking about it a good deal, I've decided that you, for the moment, are the one I'll write to and you can give all my news to the Mammy and the rest of the family. Then you can give me all of their goings on and what you're are doing as well. It was costing me my wages in writing paper and postage and you are the only one to have written back to me for three months now.

What is my marvellous news? It's a great thing I've gone and done. I've got myself another job. It wasn't that there was anything wrong with the first one, only that it was changing and the children have grown so much and no longer have need of a nurse. They are to have a governess and the eldest, you'll remember I wrote to you all about him, he's gone off to school and as a boarder the poor little dote, away from his mammy and daddy and brother and sister and him so young, but there it is. The others – his brother and sister – are growing, so they are to have a governess and that was meaning that I would have no job and that would never do now, would it?

So, I've a lovely letter of reference from Mrs Ashmede-Bartlett, where she says that I am leaving my present employment because the children are growing and have no need of a nurse and nanny and that they are to have a governess. Mrs Ashmede-Bartlett speaks most highly of me and tells me that I must keep the letter safe in case I need it for the future, which of course I'll do.

The long and the short of it is that I have another job and I was interviewed at the Ritz Hotel in Piccadilly, in London. Of course, the Mammy's sister came along with me. She thinks that no young woman is safe in London and that the entire city is a den of iniquity. She also thinks that I wear my skirts too short. She is a hundred years out of date with the fashions.

So, I am to be employed as a nurse by the Mercer family where the father is in the Diplomatic Service of England. Soon, just as soon as everything is arranged, the family is to be posted abroad and I am to go with them to France and after the family might well be moved on to Spain, if Mr Mercer is needed there. It takes my breath away, but I am to go and live in France. Now isn't that grand?

Don't let the Mammy get upset. France is further away than England, but not by much. It isn't as though I'm going to the United States of America or

Australia or anywhere as far away as that. It isn't far away at all and tell her that ships sail directly from France to Cork and that I can be back in no time at all. Remind the mammy that France is a good, Catholic country, so she won't have to pray quite so much to save my soul, as she does while I am in England.

So, give everyone in the family from the oldest to the youngest of you, all my fondest wishes and collect all the news from the family and the town to send to me in your next letter. Every day I'm waiting to hear from you.

I will be at my usual address until the end of the month, so write to me there. After I will have my new address in France to which you will have to write in future.

Your loving sister,
Ellie.

PS. What is happening with your young man? Tell me, please. I despair that I will ever be as fortunate as you and meet someone of my own.

PPS. Mr Mercer has been summoned to the British Embassy in Paris. Mrs Mercer insists that she and the children must go immediately and I will accompany them. The thought of it almost keeps me from sleeping.

1927

It was a wonderful day and I have decided to remember it forever. To help me do this, I am writing about it in my diary.

It happened years and years ago, a whole week before I was five years old. In one week's time it will be my birthday again, so that is why I remember that special day at the beginning of August.

It was afternoon and we had already finished eating our dinner. Suddenly there was a great noise outside in the street and the girl from next door came running down the back alley, shouting my name. Although she was washing up the dinner plates, Mother stopped what she was doing and came out with us into the back yard.

'What a commotion,' she said. 'Now, what is it that's happening?'

We could hear the sound of children jumping up and down on the pavement and shouting.

'Come and look. Come and look.'

And one of our neighbours said in a very breathless manner, 'Will you come and see what is happening, Mrs O'Connell. Quick. Quick.'

The neighbour took Mother's hand and pulled her out into the alley and to the corner of the street, so she could see.

'Will you just look. Your Patrick.'

We all watched what was happening and then we rushed round to the front of the house. I ran behind Mother and Dan came with me. My sister Nancy was leaning out of the upstairs window.

Suddenly, Mother stopped and clutched her hand to her throat.

'For the love of God,' she said. 'And Patrick what have you been and done? I never thought you meant to do it.'

We mustn't say 'for the love of God.' But Mother is allowed to say it at special times.

'A car,' yelled one of the boys. 'Your dah has come home in a motor car.'

I wanted to see what was happening and I pushed between the grown-ups' legs and got to the front of the crowd.

There was Father sitting at the steering wheel. He had driven the car all the way home by himself.

'Would anyone like to come for a spin?' he asked everyone.

All the children shouted that they would love to go for a ride with him and Mother said, 'Where are your manners?' And some of the children stopped to say 'Please.'

'Will you be getting in the car too?' asked one of the neighbours and Mother said, 'Only because it will be nice for Dan, with him being so young and I can't let him go on his own.'

No one asked me if I wanted to go for a ride, so I got up on the running board and stayed there. This was better as there were so many people who wanted to get in the car, we couldn't all fit in and I would have got crushed.

The motorcar windows were open and I held on tight. I took a deep breath. The seats were made from leather. The smell was lovely.

'Mrs O'Connell, will you be buying one of these next?'

Mother smiled because we were quite rich as Father was Captain of Manchester United and when he wasn't playing football, he was working at Ford's Motor Company. When he was there at the factory, he helped build the cars.

'It may be,' said Mother. 'Though Patrick has only borrowed the motor car for the day and doesn't it have a lovely shine to it?'

It was so exciting I could have gone up and down the street all day and all night, standing on the running board.

When we went round the corner, I held on at the window with both hands.

'Will you take care?' Mother called and she held on to Dan all the time, so he wouldn't fall.

'Your husband is a one,' said the neighbour and she laughed a lot. 'What will he be doing next?'

We spent all afternoon having rides in the car. We went up and down the street for hours and hours. I think Mother was a little bit frightened because she kept looking at the dial that shows how fast Father was driving. Even when Father got tired and said he was going to stop, some of us sat in the car until Father made us all get out because my brother Patrick had tried to crank the engine and start the motor. I thought it was very exciting.

Now that Father has gone away to Spain, I like to remember that day because it was beautiful and special.

We aren't rich anymore and Mother cries a lot and I know she is thinking about the lovely times we used to have and now we have to grow up without a dah.

This story is for my diary and no one else is to read it, only me.

Ellie's Letter from France
to Her Sister Mary in Ireland
September 1927

Mary, Mary

I can't wait to tell you that I now live in the very centre of Paris and yes, it is as magnificent and wonderful a city as it appears in the photographs and paintings, more beautiful, in truth. Has the postcard I sent you arrived yet? If not, there is one on its way to you and must arrive very soon.

Mrs Mercer must have told me a hundred times that she had visited Paris before. Her father was a major or some such thing and had fought in the Great War and brought the family to France to see the battlefields. The family had stayed in Paris after they had visited some of the battle sites and the cemeteries. Mrs Mercer's cousin was killed in the trenches and he only twenty-one years old. Isn't it sad? All those young men, dead before their time.

There has been such excitement and organisation for our excursions to see all the beautiful monuments. We are fortunate to live in the centre of the city and from the window of my room I can see the River Seine itself. While Mr Mercer is at work, I go with Mrs Mercer and the children to the Louvre (a famous art gallery) and the Tuileries (beautiful gardens).

Now I understand why Mrs Mercer was so very anxious to live in Paris.

I also had the opportunity to visit the Cathedral of Notre Dame. It is very impressive and is on a little island in the River Seine. Mrs Mercer insisted that I went to the Cathedral and she and the children walked along with me. When we got to the main entrance however, she didn't want to come inside, as she is a Protestant. Then she looked again and said, 'Well, it is the House of God and don't tell Robert,' and came in with me. The children were sworn to secrecy about the visit. What was she thinking? That by walking into the cathedral, she would be converted? They are strange sometimes, these people. I simple don't understand them.

Everywhere in Paris the ladies are very elegant and well dressed and everyone calls each other 'Madam,' or 'Monsieur,' and several gentlemen have called me 'Madamoiselle.' Isn't that just lovely? I do wish that people would talk like this in Ireland.

It seems likely that Mr Mercer is to receive a promotion and Mrs Mercer is delighted about this. Mrs Mercer also tells me that she is very satisfied with my work and she hopes I will stay with them for some time. What is more Mrs Mercer says that I must learn to speak the French language and that she will teach me herself. It appears that she is confident that Mr Mercer will get a promotion AND the family will stay in Paris. In preparation for my French classes and learning the language, every time I take the children for their walk, I listen to what people are saying to each other and I read the notices and messages in the shops to help me learn.

Of course, I'll write to you just the moment I know details of Mr Mercer's new job.

I must go now as one of the children is crying.

My fondest wishes to everyone from the oldest to the youngest in the family.

Your loving sister.

Ellie.

When is your young man going to England? There is certainly work for him in London.

Ellie's Letter from France
to Her Sister Mary in Ireland
November 1927

Dear Mary

What a lovely long letter it was that you sent. It was a joy to read and I have put it with your other letters. When I feel a little lonely and far from home, which I do only very rarely, then I read them all over again and get much pleasure from the reading.

It had been such a time here. The three children have been ill, one after another and then Mrs Mercer herself. SHE took ill and was in bed for a full week. I have to say that I didn't have time myself to be ill, but there, I mustn't complain as the sickness did bring an unusual benefit. With cook and the parlour maid ill as well, I had to speak French to the trades people. It is immodest to say and I would tell no one else but you, I am pleased with my new skills, though I ordered raspberry jam in mistake for strawberry jam and said something to the delivery boy from the bakery, which I thought good and correct and yet, set him laughing. It annoyed me so much I almost boxed his ears for that.

It still isn't settled what HIS new job will be, though since SHE began recovering from her illness, she speaks of nothing but staying in Paris. I fear she may be disappointed. HE says time and again that 'the decision is in the lap of the gods'. Do you think he is irreligious when he says that? Mr Mercer is not as certain as his wife that they will stay in Paris.

Do write to me soon.

Your loving sister,

Ellie.

1928

Ellie's Letter from France
to Her Sister Mary in Ireland
January 1928

Dear Mary

Happy New Year!

As the clock chimed twelve to mark midnight, I was thinking of you all. I trust that you were thinking of me. The start of 1928 and everything here is bright and festive. It is truly a season of great joy, though not everybody feels like that (I will tell you more of this in a moment).

Christmas and New Year were not quite like they are at home. Mr and Mrs Mercer tried to make it as much like Christmas in England as possible, even to ordering food and presents from the Army and Navy Stores in London.

HE also ordered a box of coloured lights. He said he had chosen them not only for the sake of the children but because of the portrait on the box. It is of a lady holding the Christmas lights in her hands, as she is just about to decorate the tree. Mr Mercer says the portrait reminds him so much of Mrs Mercer. I thought this romantic.

On Christmas Eve the children were allowed to stay up and dress the tree. It was a delightful time. I stayed with them until it was time to go to Mass. The Protestants have a church service (as Mrs Mercer calls it) on Christmas morning. The Mercers came home in time to exchange presents and to have lunch. They gave me a pair of gloves and a trim for the collar of my coat. It's most attractive and very elegant, I believe. Quite the correct thing to wear in France.

However, it seems the Mercers are not to stay in Paris after all. HE has been offered a new position in the British Embassy in Madrid, in Spain. SHE is not at all happy about this but keeps saying that she will 'put on a brave face for Robert'. Mrs Mercer keeps reminding herself and everyone else that this move is to be made because Mr Mercer had been granted an exceptional promotion. SHE tries to convince herself that the promotion is the main thing. Mr Mercer's promotion is discussed and not Paris, which now does not matter at all.

This promotion means Mr Mercer will now work in the British Embassy in Madrid and so that is where the Mercers (and me, of course) will move to next. I am led to believe Madrid is very hot in the summer and so the King and Queen and all the Spanish Court, move to Santander, as it is on the coast and much cooler. Also, I am told the Queen of Spain is English or at least she was before she married the King. Mrs Mercer tells me that the Queen is a granddaughter of Queen Victoria. I don't know whether I am supposed to be impressed or not. I suppose I am.

The staff of the Embassy and all the other diplomatic staff and other important people, follow what the Royal family do. In future I will spend my summers there in Santander. It sounds rather grand. I like Paris so very much, it is such a beautiful city. I am sad at the thought of leaving it, yet I have to say I wonder what it will be like to live in Spain. At times I am thrilled and at other times, I have to confess, I am a little apprehensive. I don't know anything at all about the country.

Before the Mercers leave for their new posting they will spend some time in England. Of course, I will travel with them, as Mrs Mercer can't manage without me. There is a good deal of arranging and packing to do and we will travel by train – First Class – to England. I fear that I won't have enough money to come home to Ireland. It seems to me so painful that I must move closer to home before I move even further away, without getting an opportunity to visit you all.

Fondest wishes to you all from the oldest to the youngest in the family.

Your loving sister,

Ellie.

PS I'm so pleased that your young man has found decent employment. Do write soon and let me know all about his new work.

Ellen's Story
Manchester
1928

She stepped back from the looking glass and ran her hands over her waist.

'Acceptable,' Ellen said to herself. 'Quite acceptable, especially for a woman who has had four children, five if you count … Well, never mind. Better than the women around here. They let themselves go.'

Downstairs there was a crash as the front door was flung open and there was the sound of steps on the linoleum.

'Mother, Mother. Are you ready? We want to see you.'

Ellen patted her waist once again. She opened the bedroom door and paused at the top of the stairs.

'Mother, you look beautiful,' said Nell.

Ellen saw her daughter looking up at her. She came down the stairs to the hall.

'You look so beautiful, so graceful,' said Nell. 'No other woman in the entire world can match you.'

At the foot of the stairs, Dan linked arms with his mother.

'Away with you,' his mother said. 'I'm only going to vote.'

'You must wear your beads with that dress,' said Dan. 'The amber ones.'

'Do you think so, do you? Well, you had better go and get them, hadn't you now?'

Dan went up the stairs two at a time.

'The top draw, on the left,' Ellen called after him.

'You're the most beautiful woman in the whole world,' said Nell. 'And when Mr Fogarty sees you, he is sure to want to marry you straight away.'

'Is that right?'

A slight creak caught their attention. Mother and daughter both turned. At the top of the stairs stood Dan. He was wearing his mother's beads and her hat. He walked down towards them, twisting the necklace through his fingers.

'What do you think?' he said. 'How do I look?'

'Stop your play acting and give them to Mother. She's in a hurry.'

'I thought I looked quite good. Never mind. The beads, they go so well with your dress. The amber of the beads, against the brown of the dress. Perfect. The dress sets them off so well.'

'Will you be letting me have those,' said Ellen. 'And the hat.'

Dan drew out the hatpin. He put the pin into the hat and passed it to his mother. 'Do you want the beads as well?' he asked.

'Now you wouldn't be expecting me to ask again, would you?' said Ellen and held out her hand.

'No,' said Dan. 'I wouldn't be doing that.' He took off the necklace and gave it to her.

'Here, Mother. Now go and vote for Mr Fogarty. He will be enchanted with the way you look and we'll have a new man in the house.'

'What do you think?' Nell said as she closed the front door. 'Do you think Mr Fogarty will want to marry Mother?'

'I'm sure of it,' said Dan. 'He can't fail to find her beautiful.'

'But there will be other women, ladies indeed, who are better dressed.' Nell said.

'No, there won't. Not around here there won't and besides Mr Fogarty is a Socialist and he will recognise mother is a Socialist too and in any case, he will see Mother, not her clothes. He'll recognise that Mother knows how to make the best of everything, even when she has nothing.'

'That doesn't make sense.'

'At a glance,' Dan continued, 'Mr Fogarty will know that Mother is poor but accomplished. That she plays the piano. That she was educated by French nuns.'

'And how will Mr Fogarty know that Mother plays the piano?' Nell asked. 'I find that difficult to believe.'

'It's obvious,' Dan continued. 'All he has to do is look at her fingers. Fine and delicate – ideal for playing the piano.'

'And that Mother was educated by French nuns?'

'Well,' said Dan. 'It's like this. Mr Fogarty will be standing outside the polling booth and he'll be calling out, "Vote for me. Vote for Fogarty," and Mother will say, "Of course, Mr Fogarty. Of course, I'll vote for you," and Mr Fogarty will recognise Mother's beautiful Dublin accent and she'll speak to Mr Fogarty so nicely, that he will know that Mother must have been educated by the French nuns, as she couldn't have been more polite.'

'I suppose. It might be like that,' said Nell. 'And will you be helping me to set the table? I'm not going to do it on my own.' She went through to the kitchen.

'It would be great to have a man in the house again,' Dan said.

'What about Patrick? He'll be twenty-one soon. He's the head of the household. Or there's you, for that matter.'

'I was thinking of someone more mature,' Dan replied.

'Ellen Fogarty. There's a good sound to the name, don't you think?'

Though, would we have to change our names, if Mother were to marry Mr Fogarty? But Father can't be dead. I'm sure he can't. I really am.'

'Doesn't count if he lives on the other side of the world.'

'Is Spain that far away? I don't know.'

'He definitely lives in Spain and he's never coming back,' said Dan.

'How do you know that he's never coming back? There are letters sometimes, at least, there were letters from Spain and Father must have sent them.'

'Can you remember when we last got a letter and besides we didn't get a letter, we only got envelopes from Spain and that doesn't count; an envelope from Spain. It doesn't count as a letter.'

'And the money?' Nell said.

'I'd not forgotten the money but that could be from anyone.'

'Oh, yes? Someone in Spain has decided for no particular reason, to send us money. To our house in Manchester. Out of kindness or as an act of charity. You believe that? I don't.'

'It's a possibility,' said Dan.

'Those letters must be sent by Father.'

'Might be, but can you remember when Mother last got a letter or envelope or whatever from Spain?'

'No,' Nell said. 'I can't remember either, but it all seems so unfair. Father living on the other side of the world, in Spain or perhaps he's dead and we don't know. At least with Mr Fogarty, he's alive and he's here.'

'Will you look at the time?' Dan said. 'Mother will be back from voting and we've not done a thing, a single thing. There'll be ructions. Just you see if I'm not right.'

Nell's Story
Manchester
October 1928

It was another of Mother's moneymaking schemes.

'There's no way it can fail,' she said. And because of that we went all the way to the other side of Manchester and made complete fools of ourselves.

Although Mother kept repeating that it was only right that four such talented children ought to be on the stage, I'm sure the imminent success in our new lives was because we have not had a letter from Spain for oh, ages.

Our father had to go to Spain to earn some money and have a good job. Every now and again he sends us envelopes stuffed with money. That means we have a wonderful time or at least we can pay the grocer and don't have to hide from the rent man. It gets difficult when Mother has spent all the money Father has sent. The last time we were refused credit at the corner shop, Dan offered to go there to recite a poem. He felt sure that his skills would be recognised and the grocer would at least let us have a loaf of bread and a quarter of tea, but he told Dan to come back with some real money and he could forget his poetry.

Nancy told Dan his idea was half-witted. She said Dan would frighten people with his poems. Dan told her to shut up as she didn't know anything about great literature or works of art.

Dan insists he is going to go back to Dublin and starve in a garret. This will enable him to write the best poetry in the world as he will have suffered and his character will be formed. Whenever she hears this, Nancy says he needn't bother to go to the trouble and expense of going to Dublin. He can have plenty of practice starving here. This only made us feel even hungrier.

Try as she might, Mother couldn't get Nancy to go to buy cigarettes for her. Nancy said we are banned from all the corner shops in a two-mile radius 'and she wasn't going any further as it looked like rain'. I think cigarettes are horrible though Mother says they help her think.

We all felt despondent when Mother remembered the notice in the newspapers a neighbour had shown her. A theatre impresario was searching for new talent. In this Mother saw an opportunity to rescue us from hunger and an early grave, as it is common knowledge people on the stage earn lots of money.

Mother had put the cutting in her apron pocket. She took it out and read the piece aloud to us. Straight away Patrick said he was going out and didn't want to be involved.

'You may regret this later,' Mother called after him.

He replied that he had an appointment and didn't want to be late.

'Get him,' Nancy said. 'So posh, he's falling over himself.'

Apparently, we had all taken the decision that we were going to the audition. I can't remember when this happened. However, once this decision was made, we were left with the problem of how to get the money for the fare for the journey. Fortunately, one of our neighbours likes us. Her only son died of diphtheria and now she thinks of us as her children. It didn't take long for Mother to persuade her the money for the tram fares was a temporary loan on our route to uncountable riches.

After that Mother declared she saw a sign, a clear sign and sent me to the bathroom to check how much soap we had left. I wasn't sure about this as a sign, though when I asked Mother all she would say was:

'The impresario will recognise the talent of you two girls and the beauty of well-washed hair.'

Apparently, Dan didn't count. He didn't need well-washed hair. A quick swill with water was enough for him. As Nancy and I have our hair washed on a Friday evenings, we look our best on Saturdays and this was the day of the auditions.

That week we learned a new expression from our neighbour: 'The boards.' We were talented and would soon be 'treading the boards.' The neighbour's cousin had worked in vaudeville until the theatre had mysteriously burned down. The neighbour said her cousin had spent years 'treading the boards.' Now we were to do the same.

As Saturday drew closer, something caused me to be a bit worried. What would the theatre impresario expect us to do? When I asked Mother, she only replied that we would need a good breakfast 'to set us up for the day.' That morning we had fried bread and tea with milk AND sugar.

In the shortest time imaginable, we were at the house and being shown into the front parlour. With a flourish, the impresario followed us into the room. I suppose that is what impresarios usually do. Immediately Mother whispered in Dan's ear and he began galloping round the room singing: 'Horsey, horsey keep your tail up.'

I was sent after him to catch hold of the ends of his scarf, so I could shake them like reins. After what seemed like an age, Dan exhausted all the verses he could remember, so we stopped. Dan neighed and shook his head from side to side and I curtsied. Then Nancy got to her feet and started to dance a hornpipe. As there wasn't a piano, Mother sang along, giving the tune quite a nautical lilt. This went on for hours and hours until Mother made it clear with a final flourish that our performance was over.

'Hey, Vera,' the theatre impresario shouted. 'Show us what you can do.'

The woman must have been standing behind the door as she came in straight away. She put her cigarette down on the mantelpiece and leaned her back against the wall. Then she lifted one leg until her toes touched the wall above her head.

'For the love of God,' Mother said. 'The woman must be made of india-rubber.'

'That's only for starters,' the theatre impresario said. Vera continued to move her legs at all sorts of strange angles to her body. She didn't show the slightest sign of effort.

'Come back when you can do the same,' the theatre impresario said.

And with that, we were shown out of the house.

On the way home Dan sat on Mother's knee.

'He'll be four next month,' she said to the ticket collector, when he asked why Dan didn't have a ticket. Mother's been saying that since Dan turned five.

1929

Patrick's Letter from Santander
to His Brother Larry in London
February 1929

Larry

We've done it! Racing de Santander is now in the Spanish First Division, though to be truthful it was touch and go on occasions.

The top national teams, namely those that have won all the appropriate cups and trophies automatically qualify. That accounted for nine teams and the tenth place was there to be decided in a one-off elimination tournament.

We were away to Madrid with so many hopes and good wishes and there we played FC Sevilla. The first goal was theirs then Oscar equalised (I tell you he is a very promising player. He'll do great things). So, a draw.

The decider was organised for two days hence. A little recuperation was granted after a strenuous match. Then one of the Spanish Royals died and the match had to be postponed. A day later and the lads were ready. It began with us scoring an own-goal (you had to feel sorry for the lad). This had the opposition ahead, then Oscar equalised for us. There were grown men with tears in their eyes. Next FC Sevilla scored again and there was a bit of trouble. Before you knew it both teams were playing with ten men. The next moment we equalised again.

This brought us to a third match and you couldn't believe the tension. It was an atmosphere to experience. Our supporters had taken over two or three bars in the old part of Madrid. They were full to overflowing and crowds spilled out on to the street. To guarantee that no one was excluded and missed out on the excitement, two slate boards were put up on the pavement. There was a telephone link to the match and every move the players made was chalked up for the crowd to see. The wonders of the modern world, don't you think?

The final score and the men erupted into cheers, hurrahs and 'vivas,' like you have never heard in your life. 2-1 to Racing de Santander. You would have loved it all, you would.

After the celebrations we caught the train from Madrid back to Santander. It pulled into the station at Reinosa, where the carnival met us and the jubilations began all over again. The crowds were out to meet us at every station onwards along the railway line and into the port. We pulled into Santander and you couldn't see the platform for men and boys and a few señoritas too. There were speeches and honours and not a few glasses of wine of the very best.

So, Larry you can understand that after more than 270 minutes of play plus a little extra time for injury against FC Sevilla and 72 hours rest interrupted by the greatest party you have ever been witness to, we were beaten in our next match against FC Barcelona. It might be that we have had too much success for our own good, but we are in the First Division and there to stay.

Raise a glass to us and to our future.

Your brother,

Patrick.

Nell's Diary
Manchester
June 1929

It's been such a busy day that I didn't expect to have time to write in my diary this evening.

An hour ago we got back home from seeing off Mother's sisters at the railway station. They have gone back to Dublin but have promised to visit us again next year.

'There,' said Mother, 'I knew that two shilling piece was waiting for something special,' when she found it in the lining of her coat. It paid for our bus fares to the centre of Manchester and back again AND for platform tickets for us all as well – that's Mother and Nancy, Dan and me. Patrick didn't come with us as he's too grown up. The platform tickets meant we were able to wave from the platform and not from behind the ticket barrier.

Dan and I suspect the florin had fallen out of Mother's wage packet when she was working at the biscuit factory. I didn't know it was possible to lose so much money and not spend the whole day looking for it.

'There was a purpose in it. That coin didn't get lost for no reason.' But Mother said that at the end of the visit our aunts made to Manchester.

Mother is a great believer in fate. The very day we got the letter from our aunts telling us they were coming to visit, was the day Toffee Jinny told

Mother extra women were being taken on at the factory where she works. As mother's sisters were coming to stay some extra money would be very useful.

The idea of working at the biscuit factory seems like heaven to Dan and I. All sorts of lovely treats are made there; biscuits and cakes and boiled sweets like fruit gums and toffee. We wondered if Mother would be able to get some of these lovely things for us like Toffee Jinny does. She is always bringing us treacle toffee and cinder toffee that has fallen to the floor and got spoiled. It seems good enough to us. I've never found any dust on what Toffee Jinny gives us.

Once Dan asked her why she doesn't eat all this wonderful toffee herself. She said, 'The smell of it turns my stomach. All that sugar and condensed milk. All day long. I've had enough of it. No, this is for you children.' Only Toffee Jinny doesn't call it condensed milk, she calls it conny onny.

I tried to imagine this but found it difficult to believe I'd ever get tired of cakes and sweets and especially toffee, however long I live. It all seems like bliss, the very idea of it.

Mother's job in the factory lasted six weeks. 'Six weeks and no more.' Mother said every evening when she got home from work. The job making biscuits meant we could have a sofa and armchairs when our aunts were staying with us. I expect the furniture will have to go back to the shop now that our guests have left, but it was nice while it lasted.

Mother's job finished two days before her sisters arrived. This gave her time to have the sofa delivered to our house and to pay some of the money we owe to the grocers. This meant we could buy more food for our visitors. Sometimes the grocers are nice about the money we own to them but sometimes they get a bit angry. Mr Harper says, 'I'm not the Charity Board, you know.'

Patrick says that means testing is an evil perpetrated by the bourgeoisie. He means that the Charity Boards check whether you have even a single penny and if you do, they won't give you any help. The grocers have no right to deny us food, according to Patrick. He says the workers are going to rise up and burn down the capitalists' shops. Though Mother did remind him that if the shops were all burned down, it would be difficult to buy food anywhere at all.

Mother says while we are waiting for the workers to rise up, we are going to look after our visitors. 'Guests in the house and we have a good meal on the table,' and, 'We are not concerned about money when family is coming to visit.' She spent all her wages so that we have a sofa to sit on and can all eat properly when her sisters are visiting here in Manchester. It's always lovely to have stews with meat in them. We all feel happy then.

We got a sofa and armchairs before but Mother couldn't keep up with the instalments and she tried to convince us that it was a blessing.

'Wooden chairs with straight backs. They are better for your posture,' she told us.

Dan said his posture was good enough already and when he's a published poet the first thing he's going to buy is a sofa and an armchair and he's going to pay for it with his royalties. Then Nancy got cross with Dan and said that if Dan intends to go to live in Dublin, he ought to remember that Ireland is now a Free State and how can there be royalties without a royal family. Dan told her she is ignorant and has no understanding of words.

If Mother hadn't stopped the two of them, I think there would have been a huge argument. She threatened to send them to bed without any supper. 'That's nothing new,' said Dan. Fortunately, Mother didn't hear this and we got to eat the bar-na-brac Mother's sisters had brought with them, as they don't think we can buy it in Manchester. It was a bit stale, though the margarine made it easier to swallow.

Now as we have paid some of the money we owe to the grocers, we will be able to eat while we are waiting for the next letter from Father. We haven't had one of those for a long time, though Mother says: 'He'll be putting the next letter in the post any day now. It takes so much time for the letters to reach us here in England and one of them might have got lost as it's a very long way from Spain.'

This is my diary and no one else is to read what I've written in it.

1930

'No, no, no,' said Dan, rearranging the sheet over his sister's shoulder. 'Remember where you are ... in Greece.'

He swept his arm round in front of him.

'Spread at your feet are fields of flowers. Behind you is the Parthenon.'

Nancy tugged at the sheet and fastened the safety pin again.

'Let Nell be Athene.'

'You are about to meet the greatest philosopher in the world.'

Dan straightened his back.

'That's me ... and he will be astounded by this vision of beauty which confronts him ... you and your handmaidens, standing in the golden sunshine of a summer's day. You are going to weave garlands of flowers to give to my students ...'

'This is a waste of time. Why can't Nell be Athene? She's better at standing still than me.'

Dan ignored the interruption.

'... garlands of flowers to give to my students, who are waiting for me in the olive groves.'

He straightened some dried grasses that leant out of a vase.

'The greatest philosopher in the history of the world, walks through the olive groves. Beyond are the Isles of ...'

'What will Mother say if she finds us up in the attic again?'

'She won't mind.'

'Will.'

'Won't. This is a drama production. I'm making you into a goddess, so you oughtn't to mind either. Just listen ... who will inspire the greatest philosopher in the history of the world, who is walking through the olive groves and then ...'

'Listen. You listen to me, for a change. It's nearly 6 o'clock and when that clock strikes, I'm going.'

'... and Aristotle is amazed at the grace of the goddess and at her profile ...'

'Her what?'

Dan turned towards the skylight and ran his finger from his forehead to his chin. 'Her profile.'

Nancy shrugged. 'I always knew my profile was something special.'

'Then the greatest philosopher in the entire history of the world will think these incredibly great thoughts ...'

Dan turned and picked up a sheet of newspaper. He rolled it into a scroll.

'... will think these incredibly great thoughts and write his greatest book. He will read it to his followers, who have been waiting for him ...' Dan glared at his sister '... in silence ...' he continued, 'in the olive groves and you and your handmaidens will weave garlands of flowers ...'

Athene jumped down from the Acropolis.

'I'm not stopping any longer. That box is broken. It's dangerous. I'm not risking my neck for you and your stupid drama any more, even if I am Athene.'

'Get back to the Acropolis. Go on. Get back.'

Dan tried to bar his sister's way as she attempted to get to the stairs.

'I'm walking through the olive groves and ...'

'I've had enough. Get Nell to be Athene. I want my tea. It's colcannon. My favourite. Can't you just smell it? It's lovely.'

1931

Patrick's Letter from Santander
to the Directors of FC Barcelona
March 1931

Sirs

It has been brought to my attention that you will shortly be requiring a new manager for the Team of FC Barcelona.

I request that you consider me for this post.

At the start of the 1922–1923 season I moved to Spain with the intension of making it my home and took the post of Manager of FC Racing de Santander. Over the following seven seasons I have managed the Team. At the end of the 1928–1929 season the Team was admitted to the First Division.

Prior to moving to Spain I played football professionally, starting my career in Dublin, Ireland and then transferring to England. I played for the teams of Sheffield Wednesday and then Hull City. From there I moved to Manchester United where I was Captain from the end of the 1914–1915 season and through the years of the Great War.

I have been awarded five International Caps and was Captain of the Irish National Team when we won the Triple Crown for the first time in our history.

I moved back to England to play for FC Ashington. After playing for the Scottish team of Dumbarton during the 1919–1920 season I moved back to England and was there for two seasons, acting as player/manager for the 1921–1922 season.

In addition to the conditions of pay previously discussed with Señor de Cossío, I request that if I am considered for the post, I receive my return ticket to my own country of Ireland, that I might make a visit there each summer.

I remain,

Yours faithfully,

Patrick O'Connell.

Patrick's letter from Santander
to His Brother Larry in London
October 1931

Dear Larry

Will you now consider me as Ireland's leading bullfighter? It was something I was tempted into over a good meal and a glass or two of the very best.

By way of a joke, the men set to commenting that Ireland would never raise a bullfighter and before you knew it, I had committed myself to proving them wrong.

It's a very Spanish sport and I can never see it gaining popularity in Dublin, Limerick or Cork but my national pride wouldn't let this challenge go without a response.

The bullfighters wear the most elaborate of costumes; an embroidered jacket and tight trousers. There was however, much hilarity as to how anything was to be found that would fit me as I am a good three or four inches taller and of a more solid build than the majority of the men here.

The mother of one of the football team is a good seamstress. In a moment I was fitted out and was ready to be on my way to the bullring. The local newspapers had made much of the event. It was considered that the novelty of an Irish bullfighter would bring in the crowds, the intention being to raise money for a local orphanage.

A football pitch at full capacity is one thing, a bullring full to capacity is quite a different matter altogether. Out of consideration for my lack of training in the sport, a very young and meek animal had been selected. Friends and colleagues had given me guidelines for what I was to do. Recalling this and what I had seen before, I twirled the cape a few times and boldly approached the animal. It looked me straight in the eye and looked as I felt. Before I knew it, I was sailing through the air and then I landed on my backside in an unceremonious fashion. The spectators found this to be hilarious. I did not. So ended my brief bullfighting career, with damage only to my dignity. It pained me I must say, to eat a stew of the creature after the afternoon's entertainment was over.

The men said that it might have been one of the briefest corridas they had attended. What it lacked in skill was however, made up for in comedy.

You will have noticed from the address, I am back in Santander after only two seasons in Oviedo. This itself is a temporary move and I must consider myself in transit. It has been indicated to me that the Managerial Post of FC Barcelona is shortly to be available and I have applied for it. Señor de Cossío has great interest in this club as well as in Racing de Santander and has encouraged me to consider this move. As a temporary measure I am acting as adviser to Racing. Whatever life has to offer, it appears I will be on the move again at the end of this season.

As ever, in great affection.

Your brother,

Patrick.

1932

'Will you be leaving that alone?' said Ellen.

Nancy gave the package another prod with her finger.

'What's in it? It's been on the hall table for an age.'

'It's Patrick's.'

'So why hasn't he opened it?'

'So will you leave it alone?' Her mother said from the sitting room.

'Why hasn't he opened it, if it's his? There might be something good in there. It's not from Spain, is it?'

'Don't be asking foolish things like that.'

'What's in it then? I'm going to open it, if Patrick can't be bothered to.'

'Leave it. There's nothing in it.'

'I'll have the string, if there's nothing in it and in any case, what is the point of making a parcel out of nothing?'

'Didn't I tell you to leave it?' her mother called. 'And don't think I don't know you are still there, miss.'

'Leave it,' Nell said. 'It's supposed to be Patrick's suit.'

'Supposed to be? If it's not Patrick's suit, what is it then?

'Don't you know? He's taken his suit to the pawn shop so often, the pawnbroker trusts him.'

'His mistake.'

'And doesn't bother to open the parcel anymore. The parcel gets pawned on a Monday morning and when Patrick gets his pay on a Friday, he goes to collect it.'

'For Saturday evening?'

'Exactly,' Nell said. 'Now all he has to do is pawn the parcel.'

'What's he done with his suit, then? Taken it to another pawn broker?'

'Are you suggesting your brother is dishonest?'

'It did occur to me he might be especially hard up at the moment.'

'He needs his suit for Wednesday evening.'

'What's special about Wednesday evening?' Nancy asked.

'He's been invited to speak.'

'Him? Who to?'

'To the workers. At the Queen's Park Parliament.'

'And he needs his suit to speak there? To half a dozen boilermakers and three navvies. In an old hut in the middle of nowhere.'

'It's Manchester's equivalent to Speakers' Corner.'

There was a pause and then Nell added, 'In Hyde Park, in London', for Nancy's benefit.

'Oh, yes?'

'Where the working man can speak his mind and discuss his beliefs.'

'They must be desperate. To ask Patrick.'

'How can you talk like that? He's your brother.'

'So?'

'And he's a worker.'

'Since when?'

'Since he got another job. With the council. And he's going to speak to his fellow workers and discuss his beliefs.'

'And then they are going to start the Revolution? I don't think. He'd never be out of bed in time.'

'He's been ground down by poverty and unemployment. His dignity has been undermined.'

'You believe that?'

'He needs his suit to restore his dignity, when he speaks to fellow workers. At the Queen's Park Parliament. Then they'll discuss their ideas and sharpen their intellect.'

'He'd better not go boozing then beforehand, if that's the case,' Nancy said.

'It was only because his dignity had been attacked.'

'So you said. But that still doesn't get me a piece of string.'

The clock in the hall chimed four.

'Is that the time?' Nell said. 'I'm meeting Dan in an hour. We're going to queue for the cheap seats. For the concert. Do you want to come?'

'Not likely.'

'There's some string in the kitchen draw. What do you need it for?'

'Never you mind. You can't do anything in this house without a major enquiry.'

'I was only asking,' Nell said, as she went up the stairs. 'No need to bite my head off.'

Patrick's Letter from Santander
to His Brother Larry in London
July 1932

Larry

A last letter from Santander before I leave for the South. It's been ten years since I first arrived here in Spain, give or take and I've been living in the North of the country from the very start, but now this is to change.

While the final details of my new job and new team are being sorted, I'm thinking of what is to be the next step in my life. It'll not be Barcelona after all I'm off to, at least not for the present. Director de Cossío has spoken well of me there and has much influence, so it remains a possibility, I might go to manage FC Barcelona at some future date.

This move takes me to the city of Seville and more precisely to the team of FC Real Betis, where the team and I will work together to see what it is possible to achieve.

I've a mind I've told you already of the extraordinary power that is Director de Cossío. It is his dream when he is not promoting the sports of football and bullfighting and extending his already extensive library, to see that every man and every woman has access to the highest levels of education and culture; the greatest minds from across Europe, indeed from across the world will gather here each year, that the ordinary man and ordinary woman might see great theatre, hear great music, enjoy great opera. Why there might even be a small place for you and your caterwauling.

Following on these magnificent plans Director de Cossío has worked with others to encourage a theatre troupe to visit Santander. It is comprised mainly of students from the University of Madrid. It is led by a young man, a certain García Something or other – everyone has two surnames here – from Granada and all the troupe have great aspirations and commitment for the future. And as for the young man, for some he is a genius, an iconoclast with outlandish ways. For others, he attacks all that is best in society, ridiculing what is pure and honourable, he sheds shame on the very traditions of Spain.

It is appropriate for me to meet this bold young man when he comes to Santander. It appears he is a good friend of the toreador, Sanchez Mejías, recent director of FC Real Betis. It would be a great honour and I must say, great advantage to meet a friend of a friend of my new football club.

My next letter to you will be from the South, from Andalucía, the home of oranges and lemons, of olive groves, of torrid passions, of the opera *Carmen* and flashing-eyed señoritas. It will be a great contrast after my many years here with its winter sea mists and heavy rains, which I have already said to you, put me much in mind of Ireland.

My new address will follow shortly.

As ever, with much affection, your brother,

Patrick.

Nancy's Story
Manchester
November 1932

'What are you doing?'

Nell stood watching her sister. Nancy continued, with great concentration.

'I asked "What are you ..."'

'And I heard you the first time, didn't I?'

Nancy sat back in the chair.

'There,' she said and held up a pair of men's boots.

'What do you think?'

'Elegant,' Nell said. 'Will you be wearing those tonight when you go to the Palais?'

Her sister nodded in the direction of the window. 'It's lashing down and my dancing shoes will dissolve, if I so much as go out of the front door in them.'

'So you'll be wearing Dan's boots, then?'

'To get there, I will. Inside, I wouldn't be seen dead in them. A pair of my brother's boots, indeed. In the Palais. For the love of God.'

She turned the boots this way and that.

'A little more in the toes and I'll be able to walk in them without falling over.'

She crumpled up another sheet of newspaper.

'The rich don't have to do this. Ever. I hate being poor. I hate every single moment of it. I hate it.'

'You should be proud to be a worker,' Nell said.

'Give me one reason why? Go on. Mind, tonight, I'm going to meet Prince Charming and he's going to take me away from all this.'

'Does royalty often go the Palais, then?'

Nancy ignored her sister.

'And he'll fall completely in love with me and bring me home in his motor car.'

'To Crumpsall?'

'Indeed. Why not?'

'And if you slip away without giving him your address, just consider.'

'What?' Nancy said. 'What?'

'It will be easy to find you again.'

'And why is that, then?'

'Think about it. And when the clock strikes twelve and you drop one of these on the steps of the palace, he won't have difficulty finding you. "Does any girl have a boot to match this?"' Nell said, in her most refined accent. '"Whose little foot will it fit? I will marry her straight away."'

Nancy gave a wry smile.

'The girl who crumples paper in Crumpsall. Married to a prince. Just think about that.'

'Funny,' Nancy said. 'Can't you just see I'm splitting my sides with laughter.' She gave the boots another quick buff. 'Why don't you come along with us? We'd have a good time. It's lovely at the Palais. It really is.'

'Jazzing isn't for me,' said her sister. 'And besides, Dan and I are saving.'

'What for? A rainy day?'

'To go to the opera. *La Bohème* is coming to Manchester.'

'Now wasn't I believing that only the very rich go to the operas?'

'The boxes cost guineas and guineas.'

'All that money to sit in a box?'

'Opera boxes. Don't you know anything? They're especially reserved for the best views of the stage. Only Dan and I will be in the gods. Sixpence with the late doors.'

'There are better ways of spending a sixpence, that I can think of.'

'For instance?'

'You'd be having a bit of fun if you came along with us.'

'Opera is entertainment and culture.'

'Sure. Listen to you. Suit yourself. Give me the Palais any day and the man who is going to sweep me off my feet, dying of love for me.'

'This evening?'

'And why not? It's a possibility. And seeing as you're going to the opera, what will you be wearing? Pearls, furs, your best silks?'

'I hadn't thought.'

Nancy opened a large paper bag. A length of material tumbled out. 'Will you look at this?' she said. 'The sewing I'm doing. Well, I estimated a little extra. A generous amount. Mrs-What's-Her-Name won't know. So, if you want a new blouse, here it is.'

The material trailed on the floor. Nell gathered it up and ran it between her fingers.

'What if she finds out?'

'She's got more money than sense, that woman. Eight yards. Nine yards. She won't know the difference.'

'It's not right.'

'And who is going to tell her? Not me, certainly.'

'It's a beautiful colour and you'd make me a new blouse? For the opera?'

'What do you think I'm offering? Why do you think I got her to buy a little extra and what with you and Patrick always going on about the redistribution of wealth, I decided as one of the workers myself, to do a little redistribution of my own, in our direction for once. Now what's wrong with that? Go on. You tell me. What's wrong with that?'

1933

Since the sofa and armchairs were taken back, we have to sit on the hard chairs again. Mother told the neighbours that the suite wasn't the quality she had expected and besides she had changed her mind about the colour. I don't expect they believed her. It's one of her favourite stories. She tells the same tale every time we have something repossessed.

We pulled the chairs up and enjoyed the warmth of a fire for the first time in days. We tried to forget that they were not as comfortable as the armchairs we had sat on only the week before. Now at least we enjoyed some heat. During the storms a tree fell over and Patrick and one of his friends got an axe from somewhere, chopped it up and brought it home from the park. The smoke curled up the chimney and disguised the damp smell in the parlour.

'There's only one thing better than wood smoke,' said Mother. 'And we don't get much peat in Manchester.'

I don't know why she says that as she was brought up in Dublin, in the very respectable part and I don't believe ever saw a peat fire once. Still, she sometimes likes to give people the impression she comes from the countryside. It's more remote and mystical.

Mother was staring into the fire. She is quite famous locally for her clairvoyance, reading fortunes in the embers. Sometimes, a neighbour will pay to hear what she has to say even though it is always about a fortune they are about to inherit or a dark, handsome stranger who will come into their lives.

Dan suddenly announced that he was giving up his job at the Imperial Chemical Industries.

'Bloody good thing too,' Patrick said. 'A brother of mine working in Imperial anything and in any case, I'm going out.' Dan ignored him and said that as soon as he could get a place on the shorthand-typing course that I go to, he's leaving the laboratories.

'It's free,' he said, 'and I'm from a needy family as much as Nell and I have to be able to do shorthand and typing because I'm going to be a writer and a poet.'

Nancy pulled a face and said no one would read anything Dan had written and beside who had ever heard of a poet from Crumpsall?

I reminded her that Dan had had a letter published in the *Manchester Guardian* and all she could say was that letters in the *Manchester Guardian* aren't the same as poems printed in books.

'And why can't Dan be a writer and a poet?' said Mother. 'Where would we be if Shakespeare's mother had insisted that he work at a chemical company or whatever they had in Tudor times? He never would have had the time to write his plays or his poems.'

Nancy shrugged her shoulders.

'Bard of Crumpsall, indeed.'

Then Dan said he's going back to Dublin and will live in a garret so that he can be inspired. 'A higher proportion of world-renowned writers are Irish than any other nationality,' he said. 'Think of Synge and of Wilde and hundreds of others.'

Everyone was quiet for a moment while we thought about this, when Mother suddenly said she could see something in the fire. The pictures were as clear as day, right before her eyes. She could see money, lots of it and was sure that father had sent the money to Uncle Larry. It was that simple; one of us had to go down to London, turn up on Uncle Larry's doorstep and he would hand over a bundle of notes which were meant for us in any case.

I was a bit dubious about this, as it all seemed a little far-fetched, though it's never a good idea to contradict Mother.

A week later when all this had completely gone out of my mind, Mother announced that I was to go to London to collect the money. I found myself starting to say, 'Which money would that be?' but before the words were out of my mouth, Mother continued, 'With the special day excursion fare and hadn't it all been meant? And the fare was ten shillings, the very last ten shillings we had in the world.' The thought of going to London was really quite wonderful, though I didn't want the others to know this, especially Dan. I reminded myself that I had lived in three countries before I was five years old; Ireland where I was born, England where we moved to for Father's football and Scotland where Father had played a season for Dumbarton, shortly before he left for Spain. I was accustomed to travel and would undertake this visit without any difficulty or problems.

The evening before I was due to go to London, Mother took me to one side.

'Will you be careful what you say to your Uncle Larry. Don't give him too much detail because he will only go telling your father and just be natural, as though you were happening to be passing by, when you suddenly thought of calling.' This seemed a little difficult, with us living in Manchester and Uncle Larry living in London, though I listened carefully to what she had to say.

'Then when you have had a lovely conversation with him,' Mother continued, 'just casually mention that we need the money your father has sent and this will remind him of the bundle of notes that has arrived from Spain.'

Before I knew it the time had passed and I was on my way to London. Mother gave me a few pennies for my bus fare. She told me that I wouldn't need more because on the return journey, I'd have the money that was waiting at Uncle Larry's. 'Don't forget on the bus, the clippie won't have change for a five pound note or even a one pound note that your Uncle Larry will have handed over to you. Make certain you have some change when you get back to Manchester.'

I spent a lot of the journey to London practising my conversation with Uncle Larry, so that he would think that I just happened to be passing by. I spent so much time thinking about this conversation that I didn't have time to read *The Ragged-Trousered Philanthropists* that I had brought with me. Dan and I had bought it through the Left Book Club. We couldn't afford it but it was so important we had decided to buy it, in any case. This was a clear statement of my political beliefs and would make the other passengers realise that I wasn't merely a provincial nobody.

The journey passed too quickly and there I was standing on the steps to Uncle Larry's theatrical boarding house near Kings Cross Station.

The door was flung open in a dramatic way and Uncle Larry burst into song.

'Which opera is that from?' he asked, before he even said hello.

'*La Traviata*,' I answered, then he gave me a hug and began calling to the Aunt Maggie.

'Maggie, Maggie, will you come here this instance?' Then Aunt Maggie hurried up the hall.

It was difficult to walk into the house. I did my best to avoid the boots and shoes and tried not to step on the newspapers, in case no one had had the opportunity to read them yet.

How could they live in such a disorganised place? How could the lodgers want to stay there? How could Uncle Larry speak to his own sister like that? Though I didn't have time to think.

Uncle Larry and the Aunt Maggie spoke over each other and I hardly understood who was asking which question.

'Tell me, Nell. How is your mother?' asked the Aunt Maggie. And before I could answer she was off to make me a cup of tea, only to continue talking to me from the kitchen, even though it was yards away at the back of the house.

'You darling girl,' she said, as she poured the tea. The cup and saucer didn't match. Mother would have been shocked at this. She was always most particular about serving food and drinks in the correct way.

'You'd like a biscuit to go with your tea, I do believe?' she said, though she never got it for me.

'Your Mother. And doesn't she have the greatest style about her? It's the little feet she has. I always say a person with the little feet can be a great dresser.' She glanced at her own feet. They looked as if they would be fine for playing football, but then I do suppose that's as it ought to be as she is father's sister.

Mother would be delighted to hear this about being considered a great dresser. She has always said father had never understood a woman's need to have style.

'What's that rubbish you are reading?' Uncle Larry asked as he burst back into the room. 'It's books like that that has the people destroyed. You're as bad as your father.'

My head whirled. I was very disappointed with Uncle Larry and I have to say that it had never occurred to me that he wouldn't share father's political views. Yet I was delighted to be told that I was like father. I always knew in my heart that we shared similar political opinions.

'Take no notice of him. It's just his way,' the Aunt Maggie said.

'He's on the side of the Reds in Spain, he is too,' Uncle Larry continued.

Immediately that comment made me feel so much better.

'Don't listen to Larry. It's his way and he's ready to take you out for something special to eat.' Then Uncle Larry rushed out into the street, with me trailing behind. His motorcar was parked at the curb. He went to open the passenger door in a very gallant manner and waited for me to be impressed. Then with much cursing and swearing as he cranked the engine he started up the car and jumped in. We were away.

What Uncle Larry didn't realise was that I had been in a motor car before. This was when father was Captain of Manchester United and he also worked as a manager in Ford's. This was his summer job, when the team wasn't playing. One day he had borrowed a car and drove back to Crumpsall in it. Everyone in the street was amazed and not a little envious. Father had spent the afternoon giving rides to the children and some of the adults too. It was such fun standing on the running board as father drove around and I can still recall the smell of the leather seats and see Father sitting at the steering wheel.

With much commotion Uncle Larry parked in front of the restaurant, saying that it was the best place to eat in town. Everything he did was loud and hurried, not at all what I was used to. Yet, despite it being the best restaurant in the town, as soon as we were inside he was complaining about the draught.

'Don't let any other customers sit there unless it is your intention that they all die of the cold,' he announced in a loud voice to the poor manager. And there was something wrong with the next table and the next. After that, I simply pretended that I wasn't with him at all. This wasn't easy and got even worse when he started to flirt with the waitress.

'What's your name, you darling girl?' Before she was able to answer he sang some verses about the beautiful girls from County Mayo.

Perhaps at this stage I ought to say that when he was young, Uncle Larry had won a scholarship and had been given proper training to be an opera singer. He was so good he had, I have been told, sung at the opening of the Leeds Theatre and Grand Opera House. Though, I have to say I didn't think the restaurant was the most appropriate place for him to practise, with all those people trying to eat their meals.

Rushing from the restaurant we were off, 'for a bit of a ride'. I tried to pay attention so I'd have details for Mother and Dan but soon I had no idea where we were. I have to confess that I did begin to daydream a little about how I might ask Uncle Larry of father's whereabouts, when I found we had stopped outside a large house. Uncle Larry rushed to ring the doorbell.

As a maid opened the front door, Uncle Larry gave a shout and dashed back to the car, leaving me to stand there alone feeling very foolish. He returned with a sack. It all seemed a little unusual to me, as people who lived in a house like that wouldn't be used to receiving anything in a sack, unless it was coal and that certainly wouldn't have been delivered to the front door.

The lady of the house welcomed us in to the front room and without opening the sack simply said, 'Thank you for the fruit.' How strange I thought. These people had so much and yet Uncle Larry was giving them more fruit than we would eat in a year.

'Who have we here?', one of the guests asked. 'Is this your latest girlfriend?'

'My niece.' Uncle Larry replied, 'Patrick's daughter.' There was no explanation of who Patrick was and it occurred to me later that perhaps these people knew my father, having met him when he made one of his visits to London. There wasn't time to think about any of these things and I would have to save them until later. The thought that these people might know my father filled me with pleasure but also with concern. Fancy my father's brother having a girlfriend and anyone thinking I might be she.

All the guests were sitting around, drinking tea out of china cups and eating dainty cakes. How Mother and Dan would have enjoyed this. The conversation flowed around me and everyone was so polite. No political arguments. No rebel songs. This wasn't what I was used to, at all.

The young man sitting next to me, put down his cup and saucer on a small side table. 'I hear you are a revolutionary, like your father,' he said. 'Don't believe that some of us here don't have revolutionary views, like you do.'

A woman laughed gently at this and when I looked at the young man's clean fingernails, I doubted that he had ever done any manual work in his life. He seemed a poor representative of the people.

'We can't be spending the entire day here. Nell has a train to catch.'

A maid fetched my coat and we were out of the house before I knew it. Uncle Larry went first, with me following behind.

As we left some of the guests spoke to me. They were very polite and wished me a safe journey home, inviting me to call again whenever I was in London. I doubt they meant it and I don't suppose they gave a second thought to my journey. It was something they considered they had to say out of politeness or some such thing. Then we were away again, back in the car and on the road once more.

All the way back to London from the suburbs, I thought how I might talk to Uncle Larry about the bundle of money Mother was sure he had for us. The idea went round in my head. What was I going to say? How could I just casually begin to talk about this money Father had sent from Spain. How was I going to be able to do it and be relaxed about him handing me a fortune. Uncle Larry had been so kind to me taking me to the restaurant for a meal and for the trip out to meet his friends, but this money from Father which I was expected to collect, I didn't know what to do. I was in a real quandary. It was very distressing.

The sack of fruit continued to trouble me, as well. Uncle Larry had bought this for his friends, when they already had fruit set out in bowls on the dining table and could afford to buy tea and cakes. They surely didn't need to put the money for food they owed on the slate until the following week, as we always have to do. The thought went through my mind that perhaps it was the money Father had sent that Uncle Larry was spending and that was how he could afford so much fruit. And what is worse, he appeared to be spending it on his friends and not keeping it for Mother, when we were so often in such desperate circumstances.

As we sped along I tried to enjoy the journey. It was all very pleasant and again I let my mind wander as we hurried through the streets.

It was only when I caught sight of a road sign for Euston Station, the reason for my visit to London came back to me with a jolt. Only a few more minutes with Uncle Larry remained to me and I would be on my way home without mentioning the money that was waiting for me to collect. Yet despite the little time remaining, I still hadn't decided how best to remind him of this.

'A fine writer of the greatest sort, though he has some contradictory beliefs.'

'Who would that be?' I asked.

'The young man who styles himself a revolutionary. You were talking to him this afternoon, I believe. The writer.'

'A writer?'

'And he didn't tell you? He generally talks of little else.'

It was scarcely believable. I had been chatting to a real writer and nobody had thought to mention it to me. If only I had known. I would have told him about Dan and the letter of his that had been published in the *Manchester Guardian*. I would have had so much more to tell Mother and Dan when I got home. What a dismal failure it had all been. Two failures in one day. A total disaster.

The car juddered to a halt.

'Well, my darling girl. It's been a joy to see you after all this time. And give my regards to your mother. What a woman for spending your poor father's money.'

It distressed me a little that Uncle Larry thought about Mother in this way. However, now was not the time to dwell on it.

'Uncle Larry,' I said, searching for my ticket to stall for time. 'Uncle Larry, have your seen Father lately?'

'Don't you go worrying yourself about your father. He's fine and well.'

'But have you seen him? Did he leave anything for us?'

The words spilled out.

'Your mother. What has she been saying now?'

'Mother thought Father might have visited you and the Aunt Maggie and,' here I swallowed nervously, 'and left us something.'

'Trust your mother to go thinking thoughts like that. In truth, your father hasn't been here for a while. Several months at least.'

I tried not to sound too desperate.

'But did he leave something for us?'

'Your father is fine and well and there is nothing more than that I can say. Now we don't want you to go missing your train, do we?'

With that I stumbled out of the car.

Uncle Larry wound down the window.

'I can't go parking at the roadside much longer. The roads are terrible crowded these days. It was a joy to see you, my darling girl and don't go worrying about your father. Come back and see us again soon. Your Aunt Maggie will be delighted and so will I.'

He turned round in his seat and took something from the back of the car.

'You'd better take this.' he said and pushed a tennis racket into my hands. Then added, 'Ten shillings, for you. Travelling can be terrible expensive these days,' before he was gone in a cloud of exhaust smoke.

I did my best not to drop the racket and it seemed fitting to fold the note and to put it in my purse. So much for the money Mother was expecting me to bring back from my visit. It was with a heavy heart that I boarded the train to return to Manchester and wondered how I was going to explain the events of the day to Mother and Dan.

1934

Young Patrick ran up the stairs two at a time and when he got to the top he skidded on the lino. He began banging on the bathroom door with the flat of his hand.

'Are you in there, Dan? Dan? Dan? Are you in there?'

He spun round to find his sister watching him.

'Where's Dan?' he demanded.

'I don't know,' said Nancy. 'I'm not his keeper.'

Patrick raced back down the stairs and through to the kitchen. Nancy leaned over the banister and shouted after him,

'That was the last time I ever lend Dan any money, ever.'

Patrick ran into the yard and flung open the back gate. His sister followed him.

'It was my shilling,' she called, as he ran along the alleyway and darted into a neighbouring yard.

'The stepladder. The stepladder. I'll be borrowing it … for Dan.'

He grabbed the ladder and half pushing it, half dragging it, negotiated it out of the yard and into the alley. A stray cat jumped out of Patrick's way. From her back step, the neighbour regarded the scene with curiosity.

'The saints in Heaven,' she said. 'What will those two boys be doing next?'

She listened as the ladder rebounded against the walls of the alley and watched as the top of the ladder disappeared from sight into the O'Connell's back yard. Young Patrick heaved the ladder into position against the back wall. Nancy stood watching. Her brother snatched at her hands and placed them on the rungs.

'Hold it steady,' he ordered. 'Lives depend on it.'

She pulled a face at his back, as he started up the ladder.

'It was my shilling,' she called after him.

When he reached the level of the window, Young Patrick pressed his face to the frosted glass. He could make out a faint shape sprawled out on the bathroom floor. He pulled his sleeve down over his clenched fingers, then smashed his fist through the window pane. Shards of glass cascaded into the washbasin.

'And I won't be paying for the new glass either,' called his sister. 'Don't think of trying to make me.'

Young Patrick pulled himself through the window and tumbled into the room. He flicked off the controls of the water heater before he bent down to his brother.

'Sit up. Sit up. Dan. Sit up, will you?' He shook Dan. His brother moved a little and groaned. Young Patrick grasped Dan under his arms and tried to prop him against the side of the bath.

From the far side of the door, he could hear Nancy.

'Let me in, will you? Let me in. You have to let me in.'

Young Patrick unbolted the bathroom door. It swung open and Nancy stumbled into the room.

'And there was I believing that you never wanted to see Dan again,' her brother said.

'It was my shilling,' Nancy said again.

She pulled the towel out from under the door, where it had been wedged and dampened it with cold water. She patted Dan's face with it. He raised his hands to his head, brushing away his sister's ministering efforts.

'Oh God. I'm still here. I didn't have enough money for the gas. Oh, God … You can't even afford to die in this house.'

And with that, he turned and began retching over the side of the bath.

Nell's Diary
Manchester
September 1934

At the time I ought to have recognised the full implications of the question when Nancy Manuel asked, 'And how is your brother, Patrick?' however, I failed to do so. Nancy Manuel had startled me. I had been absorbed in my book and so hadn't noticed her get on the bus. Reading does make the journey to and from work pass in an instant. I get so taken with the storyline, that several times I have almost missed my stop.

'And how are Dan and Nancy? And your Mother, of course?'

Then before I realised it, Nancy Manuel had sat down in the empty seat next to me.

We had been pupils together at the Girls' Grammar School in North Manchester. As we were both from working-class families, we were often thrown together. The other girls assumed we shared the same interests. As we travelled we talked about this and that. I told her about my shorthand-typing course that had led to my appointment as Junior Office Typist at the Insurance Company. Nancy told me of her part-time job in C&A's department store. In the millinery department.

Out of politeness I said that I had started to play for the local hockey team. I remembered Nancy Manuel had been a keen sports woman when we were at the grammar school. In passing I mentioned that Muriel had badly sprained her ankle and we were short of a player. Nancy Manuel said she would be happy to join us. There was nothing I could do but invite her to our house the following week, so that we could go to the playing field together.

When I told Mother she suggested we call her Nancy Manuel – her full name – so that she was not confused with my sister Nancy. It seemed appropriate. So, Nancy Manuel she was called and has remained.

When we got to the pitch I introduced her to the team coach and the captain. I told them why she had come along with me. They invited her to join the next game to assess her standard of play. What with Muriel being absent from the team for the foreseeable future and our imminent league fixtures, Nancy Manuel was offered a place in the team.

As a consequence Nancy Manuel began calling at our house once a week, sometimes twice so that we might go to the hockey matches together. Mother would often invite her in for a cup of tea. After the games she used to walk with me to the end of the street and as the evenings drew in my brother Patrick usually walked her to the bus stop. He was very considerate.

One day well into the next hockey season, I got a message from Nancy Manuel letting me know she was not feeling too well and would miss the next practice session. I was rather dismayed as we were doing well in the league and had an important match scheduled for the following week.

After all this you can imagine my surprise when I got home to find her sitting in our front room. Mother asked me to come in to join them. My brother Patrick was there as well.

Nancy Manuel was sitting in one of the armchairs we bought with the help of my first wage packet. She was looking intently at her shoes. She kept turning her feet this way and that, as if to get a better view of them from every possible angle.

Mother asked me to sit down.

'We have some news for you,' Mother said. 'Patrick and Nancy Manuel are getting married ... soon.'

At this Patrick stood up and walked round to Nancy Manuel's chair. He rested his hands on her shoulders, while she continued to examine her shoes with a great deal of attention.

'Aren't you going to offer us your congratulations?' he asked, but I couldn't think of anything appropriate to say.

This is for my diary and no one else is to read it.

Patrick's Letter from Seville
to His Brother Larry in London
October 1934

Dear Larry

I have met Ellie and I am to marry her. Do not believe for a moment my brains have been baked by the sun of Seville and that I ramble and am deluded. No, quite the contrary. I have met Ellie and she is Irish and she lives here in Spain, working as a nanny.

There cannot be above a dozen or twenty Irish women in this country and I have met one of them and we are to marry. This is a somewhat unconventional approach however, all that is past, is past. It was a different life, in a different country and what is past is finished.

Ellen, the Ellen of then, was part of the passions of youth. She and I were ill-matched, we two touched briefly, intertwined and separated. We will never meet again in this life. My children were cared for as much as was possible, given the distance and my resources. I did my best. Indeed they will all be adults, no doubt with children of their own. No more might be asked of me.

And now I have met Ellie. Miss O'Callaghan is young and lovely, a true delight and pleasure to be sure. When still in Santander I heard tell of an Irish girl, nanny to the children of a British diplomatic family. With the other embassy staff she and the family she worked for, were spending the summer months on the coast.

Friends were eager for us to meet, especially as we Irish are of such a rarity value in this country.

Her name is Ellen though you will have noticed the similarities of the name, so I have decided to call her Ellie. Less opportunity for confusion that way.

Ellie caught my attention; petite and pretty, bright and cheerful. What's more she is highly cultured, speaking French and is already learning Spanish. She is hard working – her young charges are a credit to her – and she appears to be sound and sensible with money.

We had been in each other's company several times, when I happened to meet her in the street. She was on the way to the park with the children. She said she was glad this had happened, as she wanted to say 'good bye' to me. I took this to mean that she was to return to Ireland or the family she worked for was moving on. She said that was not the case, but rather it was she who was moving on.

She had recently found a new employment working for a family of Spanish aristocrats. She would be moving to Seville. Spain suits her and she wants to remain here and she is much in demand as her spoken language is highly valued. Foreign nannies apparently are essential to the elite.

As you know my intended move to Barcelona has to be delayed. However, when the post of manager of Real Betis de Sevilla came available, it appeared destiny had intervened. It would be churlish indeed to ignore what fate has set before us.

As of next Sunday we will be married.

It is my intension to return home to Ireland via London this summer. So you will have the opportunity meet her. It is a blessing Maggie has gone back to Dublin. She would not understand and besides, as you know, she talks first without measuring her words. She would have this marriage over before it has started. It is indeed a good thing that my new wife is not from Dublin, but from another city altogether.

Yours in happiness,

Your brother, Patrick.

It is possible the manager's job at FC Barcelona will be available at the end of this season or the next. The team is doing well. What more might I want in life?

Nell's Story
Manchester
December 1934

The attic door closed behind her. Nell glanced through the banisters. A group of people huddled in the hall below. Two men were speaking to Dan in strident, urgent tones. The stairs creaked slightly as she came down to the first floor landing, then she heard the front door click shut. There was the sound of footsteps as someone went to the back of the house.

'Who was that?' Nell asked as she opened the door into the living room. 'Who was that at the door just now?'

Patrick was sitting at the table. He went on trying to assemble the crystal radio set.

'I was asking who that was at the door just now?'

Her elder brother looked up.

'Have you ever heard anything so beautiful as this?' he said. 'The BBC Northern Symphony Orchestra in our front parlour.'

'Tchaikovsky,' said Nell. 'A *Serenade for Strings*. I was asking who was that was at the door just now.'

'To think that we might listen to music like this, in our own homes. It's wonderful.'

'It's not as good as hearing it in concert,' Nell said. 'Dan and I heard the 'Serenade for Strings', at the Free Trade Hall. I was asking who that was at the door just ... oh, never mind. I'll be making some tea.'

'I think Dan has just made a pot for himself and Mother. Two sugars, when you bring it.'

Nell raised her eyebrows.

'Why is it that you can always hear me when it suits you?' she asked, as she went into the kitchen.

'Would you be wanting a cup of tea?' said Dan. 'There's plenty in the pot.'

'Who was that at the door just now?' Nell asked.

'A moment,' said Dan. 'I'll be taking this through to Mother and did you say that you'd be wanting a cup yourself? There's plenty in the pot.'

'I asked a question,' said Nell to herself, standing in the back kitchen. 'First I asked Patrick and all I got from him was how wonderful the Northern Symphony Orchestra was. Then I ask Dan the same question and all he can talk about is cups of tea. Will someone please tell me what's going on?'

'Will you hold the door open for me now for a moment,' said Dan. 'I want to give this to Mother before it gets cold.'

Nell said to herself as she let the door swing closed behind him, 'Why will no one give me an answer? Who was that at the door just now? It is a sensible, rational question. Why will no one give me a sensible, rational answer?'

1935

Patrick's Letter from Seville
to His Brother Larry in London
June 1935

Dear Larry

We've done it!

The great FC Real Betis Balonpié de Sevilla (Betis to its friends) has won La Liga. What more can a manager want than to take his team to the very top. Every man of them deserved it. It was a great moment of triumph. A singular event. Raise your glass to us. Betis is top of La Liga of Spain.

It is my plan to return to Ireland in a week or two and remain there through the summer. We will travel via London. You will be able to meet my wife, Ellie. After that I will be on the move once again. I am transferring to Barcelona for the coming season, as their new manager. Will you think of it, manager of FC Barcelona. It is my intention to take my new team to become champions of *La Liga* in a season or two. The skill is there and it is my plan to offer them the direction and the training.

Yours, in this moment of joy and triumph.

Patrick.

It is proposed Ellie's sister Annie, come and visit us when we settle in Barcelona. She has been ill – consumption was suspected. It is thought the balmy air of the Mediterranean will be beneficial for her.

Patrick's Story
Barcelona
September 1935

'You found the place without difficulty?'

Patrick sat down at the table.

His companion summoned the waiter.

'So, what do you think of our city?' the man asked. 'You have been here before, with other football teams you have managed?'

'Since my early days in Spain,' Patrick said, 'I've visited the city many times. This isn't my first visit to Barcelona.'

'The city is beautiful despite what the people have had to put up with.' The man gestured at the buildings and the expansive open space. 'This plaza is one of Gaudí's early works,' he said. 'As a young man he designed it, long before he began work on our cathedral. You will have seen La Sagrada Familia, no?'

Patrick nodded, 'An unusual addition to the city,' he said. 'This city is unique.'

'Tell me,' continued the man. 'What does your wife think of Barcelona? What is her opinion of our city?'

'It's an escape from the heat of Seville. She says we Irish were not meant to live anywhere so hot. And she enjoys being close to the sea. She's pleased to be here.'

'Good, that's good. And now you have moved from Seville, are you going to do for us what you have done for Betis?'

'That's my intention.'

'To take us to the top of *La Liga*?'

'Director Sunyol,' Patrick said, 'we've had our first training session and there is good material to work with. Excellent material.'

Sunyol nodded in agreement.

'The team will be a showpiece. Sport for All. That is my philosophy. It brings healthy people. They go together, sport and health. That is what we want to see: healthy people, playing sport. And a great football team, naturally. As a good example.'

A woman carrying a child moved between the tables. She offered a small posy of flowers for sale to the customers. The red carnations were tied with black tape. Sunyol watched her.

'What does she know of sport?' he said. 'What opportunities will her child have? As you know I'm a politician as well as lawyer and Director of the Club. These hopeless lives must to be changed. These people need, these people demand a better future. Do you know we have had men with guns patrolling the ...' He searched for the word. 'The allotments. Men patrolling the allotments, outside of this city to keep thieves away. Only desperate people steal cabbages and potatoes. It is our intention to improve their lives and one way to do this is to offer them the best football there is.'

Sunyol thrust his hand into his pocket and took out a handful of coins.

'Over here,' he called to the woman. 'Sell me your flowers and get your child something to eat. So that tomorrow the little one will be able to play sport. That's where our future lies.'

Patrick's Letter from Barcelona
to Ellie's Family in Ireland
October 1935

Dear Mary

You will excuse me writing to you rather than Ellie but I am sure that given this situation you will understand.

Ellie herself has written to you at least three times already, but her emotions have taken her and she has had to leave the letters unfinished. The telegram must have come as a great and terrible shock to you all. It is only right for you to receive this letter telling of Annie's passing and of the circumstances in which this happened.

Everyone who had got to know Annie over the past few weeks and months had begun to say how well she was looking. What good the Mediterranean sun had done to her in such a short time. What a blessing it had been that she had come to stay with us. You will be heartened to know that only last Sunday Annie walked to Mass held in the little church close to our home. She had already accepted an invitation to afternoon tea with our neighbours for next Wednesday. They tell me they wish to convey to you their condolences at the sad news.

We, none of us realised how ill Annie indeed was and Ellie blames herself for this. She was in all appearances so much better than when she arrived. Why only last week Ellie was saying how Annie had put on a little weight and how well it became her. It seemed to us both that she was making a splendid recovery and that it had been wise to suggest to her to visit us.

Let me tell you that Annie was only severely ill for a short time, less than a day, though that might make it more difficult to accept, as well as the young age at her passing.

It is the custom here especially with the foreign community, to go out for a drive on Sunday afternoons. It seems to me that I remember that there were similar jaunting carts at Howth or Bray when I was a child. It is a fine way to enjoy the sunshine with great benefit of a cooling breeze.

Last Sunday Annie and Ellie went out for a ride as usual. I myself walked down to the little cabin where the carts are hired and where the rides begin and end. It was my plan to meet them and for us all to enjoy a stroll back home.

On reaching the cabin you can imagine my great concern when I heard a great furore and learned that two foreign ladies had been killed. It is however, that sometimes people here exaggerate happenings, but I was very shocked. Then at that very moment Ellie and Annie came into view around the bend in the road. The jaunting cart had been overturned though Ellie and Annie had not been thrown out of it. Instead it was dragged along with them still trapped inside. They were both dusty and dishevelled, but otherwise apparently unharmed. Ellie wanted to order two cups of strong tea, even though she usually says that the people here do not know how to make it, as it ought to be done. Tea with lots of sugar is good for people in times of shock.

We were home within the hour and Ellie confided in me that she was concerned about Annie, believing her to be most delicate after her previous ill health. Almost as she spoke, Annie fainted away. A doctor was called immediately and ordered Annie to be taken to the hospital and of course, Ellie accompanied her. During the night Annie developed a high fever and died early the next morning.

The funeral was attended by many, both from the foreign community and from the local population. They wish me to convey their deepest sympathy to you in Ireland and that is all that I can do.

Daily, Ellie goes to leave flowers for Annie.

She will write to you shortly.

Yours, in this time of sorrow.

Patrick.

Ellie's Letter from Barcelona
to Her Family in Ireland
October 1935

My Dear Family,

You may all gain solace from knowing that Annie died in the arms of the Church – tell this to Father Eamon. I comfort myself thinking that Annie was too good for this life. She never got to be the nun that she longed be.

She never had the opportunity to give her life to the Foreign Missions as she always wanted. For that, she was taken too soon.

Annie RIP.

Patrick has been a wonderful support to me in this time of trouble.

A full and complete letter will follow.

In great sorrow at losing a loving sister and friend,

Ellie.

1936

Ellie's Letter from Barcelona to Her Sister Mary in Ireland
June 1936

Dear Mary

This is to let you know we are making our final plans for our summer visit to Ireland. You can expect us to be with you by 14th of next month at the latest. I suspect it will be a long and tedious journey by train and ship, though we must be thankful the Club meets the expenses.

It appears to be an appropriate time to leave Barcelona as the summer heat seems to be driving people a little mad. Along with the usual turmoil of the city, changes to every aspect of life and the rush to a bright future, there is a certain tension that is almost tangible. Many people have remarked on it. At first, Patrick believed it was my imagination, though more recently he admits he is inclined to agree with me. He attributes it to the fact (as he says) 'the old order never take kindly to their lives being turned up side down'. It remains to be seen what will happen here.

Our imminent return to Ireland means we will miss an event of considerable importance. You have no doubt read of the Olympic Games to be held in Berlin. Here, in Barcelona an alternative Olympics is to be held. Naturally, there is much enthusiasm, particularly amongst the young people.

This morning I heard from Patrick, groups of athletes were training at the football stadium in preparation for the event. This is an opportunity to show what the Spanish Republic can offer to the world. This is, Patrick says, an opportunity to counter-balance the Berlin Olympics that Herr Hitler is using to show his policies to such a good light.

Patrick has managed FC Barcelona to the final of La Liga. This is particularly prestigious as last season the team was in a critical position. I'm so proud of Patrick to have reversed the situation in such a spectacular way.

There is every indication the team has a great future ahead, I am delighted to report.

I must close now.

In expectation of seeing you soon.

Your sister, Ellie.

When you meet Patrick, I am sure you will like him. He is an extraordinary man and I believe, rather handsome.

Dan's Story
Manchester
July 1936

'He's done it again.'

There was a pause as Nancy waited for her comment to take its full effect.

'I said, "He's done it again." Didn't you hear me?'

'Who's done what again?'

A look of exasperation crossed her face.

'Are you listening to what I'm saying, Patrick? He's done it again.'

He put down his book.

'And I'm asking you, "Who's done what again?" if you're listening to me.'

'Dan, of course. Who else would it be?'

'What's he done again?'

'What do you think?'

'Will you tell me, then or am I going to have to guess?'

'He's tried to finish himself off. That's what he's done.'

Young Patrick sniffed.

'Can't smell any gas,' he said.

'It's not the gas, this time. It's the ponds. In the park. They're filthy, they are, and full of rubbish and he's gone and thrown himself in and tried to drown himself.'

She giggled.

Patrick shook his head. 'What is it? One moment you come telling me Dan's away drowning himself. The next you are finding something to amuse yourself.'

Nell leaned over the banister.

'What's happened? Where's Dan?'

'He's tried to drown himself. That's the second time this summer,' Nancy called back. There was a thud and the front door swung open. Dan came into the hall, muddy water oozed from his shoes. 'Will you look at the sight before us?' Nancy said, as she wiped away a tear with the back of her hand.

'It was a sight to be seen. There's Dan trying to drown himself in the ponds, when a dog jumps in, that daft little thing from the end of the street and the dog thinks Dan wants to play. The sight of it.'

'Shut up. Will you shut up?' Dan said and turned to go upstairs.

'You've got something in your hair, Ophelia,' Nancy called after him.

He snatched at the trail of waterweed and threw it to the floor.

'Just shut up.'

On the stairs, he tried to get past Nell.

She put a hand on his arm. 'Come on. You'll be needing a change of clothes.'

She leaned over the banister and called to Nancy, 'Get the bucket. You'd better mop that up. Mother is due back any moment.'

'Why me? Why is it always me?'

As she walked through to the kitchen, Nancy stopped.

'Why does he do it?' she asked Patrick. 'First the gas and now he's trying to drown himself. He's got a regular wage, in a steady job with prospects and he's going to be in that play he's been going on about for weeks, in a real theatre and he'll be a real actor on the stage. Perhaps he'll even be a Hollywood film star one day, that's if he doesn't finish himself off first.'

She thought about this for a moment. 'Hollywood. All those stars; Gladys Cooper, Gary Cooper, James Gagney. I like him. He's Irish.'

'Might be,' Patrick said, 'but will you get on with whatever it is that you're doing.'

'Do you think I could go and make Dan's costumes, that's if he gets to Hollywood?'

'Ask him,' said her brother. 'Ask him, not me.'

'There must be hundreds and hundreds of girls making all those costumes, for the film stars. What do you think, Patrick?'

He put down his book again.

'Come the Revolution,' he muttered.

'And the dog was barking and splashing around and Dan was clinging on to the plank and the owner ....'

Nancy was laughing so much she found it hard to continue. She took a deep breath and went on. 'And he thought Dan was trying to rescue the dog and he was running up and down the bank, shouting that the dog could swim. Talk of Laurel and Hardy. When you think of it, who needs Hollywood and all those film stars, when we've got this on our own door step.'

Nancy looked at her brother, 'What are you doing here?' she asked, 'Oughtn't you to be at home with your wife and the babies, that's if you haven't got a job to go to?'

Her brother put his book down on the table. 'I came here for some peace. A vain hope, indeed it was.'

Nancy gave him a forced smile. 'Why does he do it?' she asked.

'He's got his own problems,' Patrick replied. 'And so will you have, if you don't get the mop and bucket before Mother gets back.'

Patrick's Story
Barcelona
August 1936

As Ellie came into the room she took a package out of her shopping basket.

'Soap,' she said and held it to her nose. 'And it's fragranced. That stall in the market. I don't know how they manage to get these things.'

She put the basket on the table and leaned over to turn down the volume of the radio. 'I know you like that announcer and her programmes. You've said so a dozen times. She's so enthusiastic and very popular with everyone, but it's very loud.'

She held the soap to her nose again. 'Mind you, not that it was cheap but sometimes ...' She stopped for a moment. 'What's the matter? Patrick. Something's wrong. What is it?'

'We've had a telephone call,' he said.

'I don't understand. What was wrong with the call?'

'At the stadium. From Madrid.'

'What's happened?'

'He hasn't arrived.'

'Who hasn't arrived?'

'Sunyol. Josep. He hasn't arrived. He hasn't got to Madrid.'

'Why should that matter?'

'You know what's happening? To this country? There's an uprising. To overthrow the Government, the elected government.'

'Don't worry. He'll be fine. He's late. Sunyol, he's been delayed, surely. He'll be fine.'

'He ought to have been there hours ago.'

'The car's broken down. They've got lost. I don't know. He might have been taken ill. Any number of things might have happened. You know what those cars are like. Always problems with them.'

'In the area, heavy fighting's been reported. The area he was due to drive through. The Nationalists. They've broken through.'

'Are you sure?'

'On the road. The road he'd travelled along.'

Ellie sat down. 'His poor wife,' she said. 'She must be frantic. His little boy.'

'It doesn't bode well,' Patrick said. 'It seems there's been shooting. Bodies were reported lying by the side of the road by a car ... but who knows what's happening. Nothing's been confirmed.'

'They must be so worried. His wife and his little son.'

'Someone's gone over to their home, to see if there is anything we can do for them.'

'I've seen his car,' Ellie said. 'It's got diplomatic plates, hasn't it? Surely those would be respected?'

'All you need is one fanatic with a gun.'

Ellie took a deep breath. 'It doesn't bear thinking about,' she said.

They sat in silence for a moment.

'Has anyone called the hospitals? There might have been an accident. The car might have gone off the road. I don't know. It doesn't have to be something so terrible. Any number of things might have happened.'

'A lot of the telephone lines are down. Someone at the club is trying to get through to anyone he can think of, who might have some sort of information. Anyone who might know what's happened.'

'Just you see. He'll have had an accident. Something will be wrong with the car. He'll be alright. I'm sure he will.'

Patrick stood up. 'I've got to go back to the stadium. To see if there is anything I can do. To see if there is any news.'

'Josep. He'll be fine,' said Ellie. 'Just you see. I'm sure of it.'

'Let's hope you're right but I've got to get back. I can't stay here.'

'Take care,' said Ellie. 'In the name of God, please take care. I'll pray for you and for Josep.'

1937

Ellie's Letter from London
to Her Sister Mary in Ireland
April 1937

Dear Mary

I've got something of tremendous importance to tell you. I can scarcely believe it myself but I'm expecting a baby. After all these years of marriage and now at the worst possible time with this beautiful country collapsing around us – I am having a baby.

It is something I never expected to happen that Patrick and I would become parents. Why by the time the child becomes an adult, Patrick will be over seventy years of age. Imagine.

Secretly, I've been considering names for the child. If the baby is a boy, I favour 'Patrick' but what ought we to call the child if it is a girl. Ann perhaps in memory of Annie? I don't know. Patrick says another 'Patrick' would be confusing and neither will know who I am speaking to. Never mind, there is plenty of time to decide.

As the situation here is getting worse by the day, Patrick believes I ought to go as soon as possible. I am reluctant to leave at this special time as it is even more important for me to be with him. It is comforting to know that in my present condition I would have priority for a place on one of the naval ships taking people out of the Republic.

Despite the difficulties and now that Patrick's salary has been reduced to 1,000 pesetas a month – as the club has very little money at the moment – he does his utmost to ensure I eat as well as possible. There are extra food allowances for expectant mothers and I am benefiting from these, though I must say I never did like cod liver oil. This appeared in abundance for a short time, though thankfully has now disappeared again from the medical centres.

It has always seemed to me Patrick suffered a great loss in his life before I met him. It is never my intention to pry but if ever I even elude to this time before I met him, he becomes quiet and we go no further. Let's hope the baby makes up for this in some small way.

Goodness, my mind is full of searches for wool and knitting needles, of where the baby will sleep and if it is possible to get any toys. I never realised these simple things could be so exciting.

I hope you share our joy at this unexpected event.

With much love

Ellie.

Ellie's Letter from London
to Her Sister Mary in Ireland
May 1937

Dear Mary

Firstly, I must ask you to excuse my handwriting but I am still shaking from head to foot. Indeed, I must ask you to excuse my writing to you at all after the events of the day. It is not my intention to distress you, but it is better I am occupied rather than let myself dwell on what might have happened and how it might have turned out.

I do not wish to worry you, yet I must be realistic. The city is in chaos to such an extent even the most simple and basic tasks take time and preparation beyond anything we might have believed a year or two ago.

This morning I caught one of the rare buses into the centre of the city with the intention of buying a few poor things I had heard were on sale there.

At the moment needles and thread are worth their weight in gold, as so many of the shops have been damaged during the fighting and the stock has been destroyed. Everything has to be mended ten times over. This fighting, by the way, is between one group within the Republic and another group within the Republic, each as the true saviour of the people.

Patrick says if they continue to fight each other like this, they will guarantee a victory for Franco and his Nationalist armies. I digress. The few wares available are set out on trestle tables on the pavement for the customers to see. So many of the buildings are too dangerous to enter, as often they have been flooded by the water used to put out the fires or they are dark as there is no electricity for lighting them.

Together with a group of local women I was examining the goods when shots rang out. Needless to say, we all scattered to take cover. One of the women became separated from her daughter – a young girl of seven or eight years of age. When the shooting stopped the child was lying in the street, her head in the gutter and her feet on the pavement. The poor woman screamed and screamed and was completely hysterical, the like of which would have broken your heart.

Between us we held back the woman as she wanted immediately to dash into the street to rescue her daughter. Someone who knew her reminded her of her other children waiting at home. They could not do without a mother. We waited to see if there was to be any more shooting and when it seemed to be quiet, we crept along by the wall. One of the women waved a dish cloth she had just bought. She said that at a distance it would look like a white flag and we would not be shot at. We kept as close to the wall as possible until the last moment and then moved out to the gutter.

Thanks be to God. We managed to move the child to the safety of the entrance of a block of flats and miracle of miracles the child was only concussed and had a nasty gash on her head but nothing more. She must have fallen as we all fled and to our great relief, the bullets had missed her.

The woman was distressed beyond words and could not believe the child was alive, until she held the little girl in her arms again. It was a delight to see them once they were reunited. The woman took her daughter in her arms and repeated, 'She's alive. She's alive,' a hundred times over and rocked her like a baby. A true pleasure after a terrible start to the day. I left as soon as it appeared to be safe and do not intent to go back into the centre of the city until all this has calmed down.

Thank God the child was unharmed.

Each time however, I close my eyes I see the little girl lying in the street, her lovely, yellow dress splashed with blood. The bow from her hair floated in a pool of dirty water. And I think of how this might all have ended. It seems now to be so foolish for the woman to have been waving a dishcloth, but at the time it seemed essential.

Enough. We are safe and have sufficient to eat. From the bottom of my heart I hope our baby never has to face anything similar to this dreadful war as he or she is growing up. These are trying times for us all.

Say a prayer for the little girl and her safe recovery.

If I don't answer your questions in a logical way or repeat myself two or three times over, you will understand why.

One last thing. I must tell you Patrick will soon be away with the FC Barcelona team. They begin a tour of Mexico and then on to New York, whenever the necessary paperwork is completed and the visas have been issued. This tour will show the world the Republicans are not a swarm of fiends and that they, the footballers, are sportsmen who come as Ambassadors of Goodwill and are sane and kindly men.

It is also the desire of these men to raise some money to allow the team to continue beyond this terrible war. They have been offered a wonderful opportunity to do this. They go on this tour after an invitation from a businessman, a certain Sr Mas Serrano, who used to follow them closely. He emigrated to Mexico and there continues his interest in his beloved team. He knows of the difficulties it and the entire country is going through at present and has organised the tour to offer some help.

Patrick has tried to persuade me to leave the country before he sets off on the tour. He says he will be less concerned about my welfare if I am in London or at home with you all. However, I still have my work at the Red Cross and believe I am needed here, at least for a little time longer. We will review the situation when Patrick returns. We have however, agreed that for now we will keep our secret to ourselves.

Patrick tells me a neighbour has arrived with some camomile tea for me. This is to soothe my nerves and help me sleep after the events of the day.

This letter will be posted in London. A thoughtful young man who was serving in the International Brigades has offered to do this for us. The young man was badly wounded at the Battle of Jarama of last year and only now is sufficiently restored to health to travel back to England.

Your last two letters arrived on the same day, though they were written a month apart. Some of the post has taken five or six weeks to reach us and the postal service itself is in total chaos as you might imagine. Please do not let this stop you writing to me. You can't imagine how I value each and every letter.

I must close now.

Your loving sister,

Ellie.

Patrick's Letter from Barcelona
to His Brother Larry in London
May 1937

Dear Larry

It is certain that we leave on the Tour within the coming week – the 22nd or 23rd at the latest. We have to travel through France as it is now impossible for us to go through northwest Spain, as it has fallen to the Nationalists. The route we must take is along the Mediterranean coast, over the frontier and then across the country to one of the Atlantic ports – almost certainly to St Nazaire, where we embark on a liner to take us to the Americas.

This beautiful city is a veritable maelstrom, with groups of people rushing here and there, shooting at each other and accusing the others of betraying what we all are seeking – namely, the defeat of fascism. Rumours sweep around as to what is happening at the main telephone exchange in particular and yet people try to continue with their lives.

Day by day the situation gets worse.

People are flooding into the city and in the west Bilbao on the Bay of Biscay has fallen. Whispers say that we, the team and administration staff, are fleeing and some of the men have taken this very badly. Our supporters tell us that we are the true Ambassadors for the Republic. We are the representatives of the elected government. Every match we win will show the world what the Republic is made of and help win the fight against Franco and his armies. The team is ready. The cases packed and we have just heard our physiotherapist has been called up. Here, you have to expect anything and everything.

With a little persuasion, Angel – a fine athlete and grounds man – has agreed to come with us on the tour. He's a good lad and very keen. He attended an athletic meeting in Paris and there, saw the benefits therapy might offer to sportsmen. I've said to him that as he can get the best from the turf, he'll be able to get the best from the men as well. It may be that all those injuries I suffered over the years were to serve a purpose. I'm an expert on the receiving end of physiotherapy and am taking books with me. What Angel doesn't know, we'll cover on the journey.

Ellie knows this will be a long separation. This fighting means nothing may be depended upon. If it is impossible for me to return or the warring prevents this, I ask that Ellie may come to you. I know you will not turn her away. She would eventually make her way back to Ireland, though in London you are her help and her support. At this stage, she is not sure if any of her family has remained in Britain.

Last evening we strolled home from the cinema. We heard gunfire in the distance and there have been more bombings in the city. Yet we enjoyed the film and had as good an evening's entertainment as ever we would in Dublin or London. The world is a strange place.

Our neighbours leave for France tomorrow and then for England. They plan to settle there until this trouble is over. They have assured me that they will post this letter to you as soon as they arrive. The postal service here scarcely exists. If any of these letters reach you, it will be good fortune indeed.

Your brother

Patrick.

Every day I am off to the British Consulate to get my papers in order for the visit to Mexico. The Consulate has taken over responsibility for Irish Affairs in this time of difficulty. It is a tedious thing but this is what happens when you live in one foreign country and want to visit a third place. Papers to leave, papers to enter, visas and passport stamps. The list goes on but they are all essential if I am to manage this tour. When I was last there the Consul told me he had received a letter from Manchester inquiring after my wellbeing. Will she never give up?

Patrick's Story
Barcelona
May 1937

'Good lad, Angel. Good lad. Rising to a challenge. Watering the pitch with a trickle of water and a hose like a sieve. If anyone can do it, you can, Angel. You're a good lad.'

For a moment Patrick continued speaking as the young man went on with his work.

'That's a grand job you're doing,' he called. 'Keep on with it. There was water for a full hour yesterday.'

The young man concentrated on the task before him. 'It'll be fine. I promise it. The pitch. In time for the match.'

He swung the hose across the mouth of the goal. 'Keeps the dust down, as well.'

Patrick looked at the pitch.

'I've been noticing. You're able to get the best out of things, even in difficult times.'

'I like to think so,' the young man said.

'And from people, too. You manage to get the best from people, even in these troubled times. I've heard what the men are saying about your therapy skills.'

'Glad to hear it.'

'Physiotherapy, massage. Your fame is spreading.'

'Just a few tips. Things I've learned at the athletic competitions. Many of the athletes use the new therapies all the time.'

'Therapy. It works for footballers too.'

'I've helped some of the team. When they come to me, but they've got their own therapist, the team masseur.'

'He's been called up.'

'Who has?'

'The masseur.'

'I hadn't heard. When does he leave?'

'End of the week.'

'I didn't know.'

'So we'll need a replacement.'

'What can I offer? I've learned a few things. That's all. It's not as though I've got any training. I've seen the work the therapists do. Benefitted from it as well. Nothing more than that.'

Angel shrugged. 'I don't wish to disappoint you but I've had no real training. That's the truth.'

'Listen,' Patrick said. 'You know enough and what you don't know, we can work out between us. We'll get together a few books and study them. God knows I've had enough injuries in my time. I know what works. Believe me.'

The young man paused.

'You think I'm able to do this?'

Patrick nodded. 'Would I have asked you, if I had thought otherwise?'

'If that's your opinion, Manager O'Connell, then I'll try. I can't guarantee anything, but I'll try.'

'Excellent. Excellent. We'll work on this on the way.'

'On the way? Where?'

'Didn't I say? Now, there you go. Absent-minded of me. On the way to Mexico.'

'Mexico?'

'Beautiful country, I hear and ardent supporters of FC Barcelona and the Republic. What do you say? At no cost to yourself. All expenses paid.'

'It's not that.'

'You've not been called up have you?'

'No, no. But will I be able to leave? Will I get permission?'

'No trouble. It's sorted.'

'You've got permission already? For me?'

'A little preliminary investigation.'

'And?'

'We go as Ambassadors for the Republic. Ambassadors of Sport. What do you say?'

Angel glanced down at the hose.

'Water's off again,' he said. 'Had more yesterday. Mustn't complain. If you believe I can do it, Manager O'Connell, I'll give it my best.'

He drained the last of the water on to the pitch and rolled up the hose.

'There's one other slight difficulty,' he said.

'The journey. The food. They are all paid for, more or less, by Sr Serrano.'

'No, it's not that, well it's that too, but there's another difficulty. I don't like to say but I don't have a suitcase or a suit for that matter.'

'The Mexicans aren't expecting a fashion parade. They know there is a war being fought here. We'll find a suitcase for you and a suit. No problem.'

Patrick offered his hand to the young man. They shook on the proposal.

'You're part of a team, a great team,' Patrick said. 'And that team is going to win.'

Patrick's Story
Barcelona
May 1937

A cheer went up from the team members as Angel walked along the platform. He set his suitcase down and gave a deep bow to Patrick.

'Everything's organised,' he said to the manager. 'I've got my suitcase and I've got my suit. I'll be the best physiotherapist that any football team could ever have.' He clambered into the carriage.

Patrick joined Administrator Rossend at the open window. There were flags flying at factory windows. He read the slogans they carried. 'Production increases day by day. We surpass our targets. No pasaran.'

'Well?' said the administrator. 'Are we Ambassadors for Sport or are we leaving the sinking ship?'

'Rossend, we go as Ambassadors for Sport. Every time. Ambassadors, that's what we are,' Patrick replied.

'You believe that?'

'What else would I believe?'

'Have you seen the note one of the lads found tucked inside his football boot?'

'What's that?'

'That we're fleeing. That we'll never see this country again. That we don't deserve to return.'

'Sport is above politics and besides, we didn't rise up against the elected Government.'

'Careful,' one of the footballers called to Angel.

'People will think that you want to travel First Class on this train, when you're dressed like that.'

'First class, who needs that. We've got something better,' said one of the other footballers. 'Three seats and three metres of floor to sit on. The lucky ones get the suitcases to lean against.'

Angel got down to the floor and leaned against his case.

'What have you brought to eat?' he asked.

The other men opened the paper packages they'd brought.

'Bread. Bread. Bread and tomato.'

'That makes a pleasant change.'

'Hey. What's this?' someone said. 'A tin of sardines. Who's got connections? Where did you get that from?' He held up the tin for the others to see. There were murmurs of admiration.

Administrator Rossend watched the group of footballers. 'I'll take care of that,' he said as he gathered the food together. 'We don't want anyone having more than their fair share.'

'That's unlikely,' said one of the players.

Passengers leaned out of the open carriage windows, speaking to family and friends. The train started to move. People walked along the platform, continuing conversations as the train gathered speed, talking until the last possible moment.

A woman called up to one of the footballers. 'Don't forget, "They will not pass."'

'Don't worry. Grandma. Everything'll be fine.'

'They will not pass,' she called out again and wiped her eyes with her scarf. The train moved out of the station.

'Only one hour and twenty minutes late, setting off,' said Rossend. 'Things are looking good.'

'We aren't fleeing,' said Patrick.

'This isn't your country. You're in someone else's war. Doesn't that trouble you?'

'Sport, that's what we are here for. Let's keep it that way,' one of the team interrupted.

'Want to join us in a game, Manager O'Connell? Balmanya's brought a pack of cards with him. It'll pass the time.'

The men sat on the carriage floor. Balmanya shuffled the deck of cards.

'No gambling,' an elderly passenger shouted. 'Bourgeois pastime. No room for it here in our new, clean society.'

'Who said anything about gambling, Granddad? We've no money to bet with.'

Balmanya continued to run the cards from hand to hand. 'Tell you what. The winner gets the tin of sardines.'

'I thought we were sharing the food. What's the point of winning a tin of sardines, if we're only going to share it? Seems senseless to me.'

'Makes it more interesting that way. Only the winner gets to donate the tin. You get to give the tin of sardines to the team. You win. I win. It makes it more interesting when there's a winner.'

There was a groan from the other players.

'For a tin of sardines, we are going to share?' one of the footballers said.

'Got a better idea? Manager, please. You present the tin to the winner. British sense of fair play.'

'British?' said Manager O'Connell 'What have they got to do with it?' One of the players tossed the tin to Patrick. He caught it and put it in his pocket.

'But I thought ...' one of the team said.

'Winner takes all.'

Patrick turned back to look out of the carriage window. 'The sea's calm today,' he said.

Patrick's Story
Travelling Towards the Frontier with France
May 1937

The explosion rocked the train. Passengers pitched forward, stumbling over each other.

'Watch out. Cover your heads,' one of the passengers shouted out.

'Glass. There's enough to cut your skulls in half.'

'Take care everyone,' another shouted.

Balmanya picked the splinters out of his hair. 'The bastards,' he said. 'They've seen us. There's a frigate, out there.'

He turned to look down the carriage and spoke to one of the other members of the team. 'Mur. Over here, quick. Come and help.'

Patrick was leaned heavily against the carriage wall. He pulled a handkerchief from his pocket and dabbed his face. 'It's nothing,' he said.

The train lurched again and Mur dropped to the floor, close to where Patrick sat. 'Are you able to move your arm?' he asked. 'Show me.'

Patrick flexed his elbow. 'A week ago, Angel, you were telling us you knew next to nothing about therapy. Now you're halfway to becoming the team doctor.' He opened and shut both his hands. 'See. Nothing broken. Go on, see how the others are.'

The train jolted forward once more.

The elderly man stood up. 'Death to fascism,' he shouted and raised a clenched fist.

Mur grabbled his arm. 'Get down, Granddad. It won't help the war effort if you go and get yourself killed.'

The elderly man sat down with a thud and waved his fist in the direction of the frigate. 'Where did you get all those weapons from? Go on. Tell us,' he shouted.

'Will someone explain the ways of the world to this old man?' Balmanya said and shook his head, in mock disbelief. 'This is non-intervention and non-intervention means that they have lots of new weapons and nice, big ships and lots of new aeroplanes and we haven't. That's the way of the world.'

Mur reached under a seat. 'Manager O'Connell. This is yours, I believe.' He picked up a trilby hat and brushed it with his sleeve. He handed it back to Patrick. 'You're going to need this when we get to Mexico.'

Patrick's Story
Close to the Frontier Between Spain and France
May 1937

The bombardment continued for more than an hour. As each mortar hit the ground, a cascade of rock fragments came tumbling down the face of the railway cutting.

Patrick walked back along the track and stopped to speak to Rossend. 'I've spoken to the engine driver. The shelling generally stops at dusk.'

'We get away then?'

'That's what this mob expect us to do.' Patrick nodded in the direction of the ship. 'No, we'll stay here for a few hours after nightfall. The frigates patrol the coast and lob a few shells in our direction. They think we'll make a dash for the frontier as soon as it's dark. We stay here longer, they get tired of waiting and clear off.'

'And we'll get away before day break?'

'That's the idea and then, we are over the frontier and into France. The worst is the last section. The railway line's right by the beach. Almost on the sands. The engine driver does this run regularly. A few hours and then we'll ...'

A woman interrupted the conversation between the two men. She held a large piece of wood in her hands and was attempting to pass it out of the carriage window. 'Here, comrades. Take this.'

'One of the advantages of travelling third class,' Rossend said. 'It's never uninteresting.'

'Indeed,' Patrick said. 'Sheltering in railway cuttings and breaking up the railway carriage. The richness of life.' There was a loud crack as the back of another seat came free. A young boy cheered in triumph.

'It takes people's minds off the bombing,' the woman said. 'Here, catch this.' She swung the back of a seat out through the carriage window. 'Careful, every piece counts. I've got two pregnant women here and a child with bronchitis. They need a bit of warmth. It gets cold at night. Even at this time of year.'

She continued passing pieces of wood down to the two men. From inside the carriage came the sounds of more seats being broken up.

The woman stopped and put down a large piece of wood. 'What's that?' she said to Patrick and pointed at his jacket. 'What is it? What have you got there in your pocket?'

'A tin of sardines,' said Patrick.

'Black market?'

'No.'

'Does it belong to anyone?'

'It belongs to the football team.'

'Let me see.' She held out her hand for the tin. Patrick passed it up to her through the open window.

'Held in common by the team. Ask them. Not private property.'

The woman nodded. 'Good enough,' she said. She went to pass the tin back to Patrick.

'You keep it,' he said. 'There are others who need it more than we do.'

The woman fed the wood onto an impromptu bonfire, then she turned to Patrick once more. 'Where are you going?' she asked.

'Mexico,' Patrick replied.

'There is a war being fought against fascism and you are going to play football in Mexico?'

'We're Ambassadors of the Republic, Ambassadors for Sport. This is an official tour. Sanctioned by the Government,' he replied.

She nodded again, then wiped her hands on her overalls and hauled herself back into the carriage. 'Come on, comrades. You can help me build the fire. They can't see it from here as long as we stay in the cutting. No one from this carriage is going to suffer from cold, not while I'm here,' she said.

Patrick's Story
The Frontier Between Spain and France
May 1937

'Hey, come and join us.'

Patrick and Rossend moved aside to let the young man get through the carriage door.

'What's happening?'

'We'll be here for hours yet,' said Mur. 'Stowaways. French Immigration suspects there are stowaways. There are on just about every train that comes this way. We'll be kept here for hours.'

'I've had enough of this,' Ventolrà said and tried the handle of the carriage door. It swung open and he dropped down to the ground at the side of the track. 'I'll see if I can find out any more. Don't let them go without me. I'm indispensable to the team. You can't manage without me.'

Passengers watched the young man walk back along the track. More carriage doors swung open. Other people followed his lead and clambered down to join him.

'Under normal circumstances, we would arrive in Paris tomorrow morning,' said Mur.

'Normal circumstances? What are they?' Balmanya asked.

'Before the war, I did this journey,' said Mur. 'I went to the Athletics Championships in Paris. A year or so ago, I was there at the Championships and I saw physiotherapy in use.'

'And you're going to be our physiotherapist? For the team?'

'At the Championships. The therapists were very good. They helped the players. It works. I've seen it. And now our therapist's been called up. Someone was needed for the job and Manager O'Connell asked me to join the tour. He tells me I'm enthusiastic about therapy and so here I am.'

'Not a bad start to a career.' said Balmanya, 'A tour of Mexico and all those beautiful señoritas and that lovely, lovely food and they're on our side.'

'The señoritas?'

'Who knows. We can only hope. I was talking about the Mexicans.'

'Won't they support their own teams?'

'The Republic. Support the Republic. Wake up, man. Where have you been for the past year? The Republic, the Mexicans support the Republic.'

'Right. Right. Politics, right.'

A group of French officials gathered at the back of the train. Several bent to look at the underside of the carriage,

'There's one here,' a man shouted and tugged at a ragged jacket that trailed between the wheels. 'Don't let him get away.'

The boy of twelve or thirteen dropped to the ground and took off along the railway track. A cheer went up from some of the passengers.

'Something I don't understand.'

'What's that, then?

'What will there be to come back to? No Republic. No country. Nothing.'

'Defeatism.'

'Just look around you. Look what's happening. It's not 'if', it's 'when' the Republic falls. It's only a matter of time. The rebels are going to win.'

'That's defeatism.'

'Realism. It's realism.'

Balmanya took a deep breath.

'At the frontier, when we crossed into France.'

'And?'

'I swear I saw Manager O'Connell, with a British passport just now, but Ventolrà says he's Irish. What do you make of it?

'Ask him.'

'I have done and he answered me and after, I understood less than I did before. Mind he's a good trainer. One of the best. That's why Sunyol brought him to the club. Remember what Manager O'Connell did for Real Betis. Took them to the top. Won *La Liga* and soon he'll do the same for us.'

'It's too late. The whole thing's going to fall apart.'

'The League?'

Balmanya slammed his hand down on the wall of the carriage.

'No. The country. By the time we've finished this tour, there'll be nothing left for us to come back to.' He thought about this for a moment. 'Fancy another game of cards? I wonder if Manager O'Connell's still got the tin of sardines. I'm famished.'

Extract from
the *Irish Sportsman* Newspaper
May 1937

From Our Paris Correspondent

Didn't the Irish team play a great game? They gave a very creditable challenge to the French in today's match.

A few questions will be asked about the penalty awarded in the fifty-ninth minute and that corner will not be forgotten in a hurry. Overall however, we have to say that the final score did justice to a great game.

And after it was over and we were back at our hotel, taking a well-earned rest and a little light refreshment, what happened but Patrick 'Connie' O'Connell, our old friend and International player, (capped six times for Ireland), walked into the bar and introduced himself to the present company.

Some of our readers will recall Connie's early days with the Dublin teams, Stranville Juniors, Francfort and later, with Liffey Wanderers, before he left us to join Belfast Celtic and then to move on to play for a number of English teams; Sheffield Wednesday, Hull City and Manchester United.

It was with a touch of bad luck that Connie's playing days were at their height – he Captained Manchester United in the 1914–1915 season and throughout the conflagration of the Great War, the League system over in England was closing down for the duration of this terrible event. By the time it was over well, we were all a few years older.

The twists and turns of fate introduced Connie to a new career. He's already managed several well-known clubs in Spain: Racing de Santander, FC Ovievo and has managed the Seville team FC Real Betis, to the very top of the First Division for the first time in their history.

Now Connie's with FC Barcelona and is managing the team on their fundraising Tour of Mexico and USA.

Any of you out there who happen to pick up a copy of this newspaper in the USA – watch out for Connie, as he is due in New York with the FC Barcelona team, later on in the year. As Connie says, he's always delighted to meet up with old friends, especially those of you from the footballing fraternity. Come along and add your support when FC Barcelona is playing so far from home.

Spain is in a bit of turmoil itself and the team of FC Barcelona is bound for Mexico as Ambassadors of Good Will for the Republic. The team sails from St Nazaire and has a brief stop over in Havana, Cuba. The lads will be undertaking a rigorous training programme, directed by the man himself, Connie O'Connell. This will prepare them for the intensive series of matches they are to play in Mexico. The team plans to raise a spot of much needed cash as they go, as well as getting all that support.

Good luck, lads! Come on FC Barcelona!

Patrick's Story
Nearing the Coast of Cuba
June 1937

The ship rolled a little. There were a few shouts of alarm. One or two passengers clung to the ship's railings.

'Some of the lads haven't got their sea legs yet,' Rossend said, as Patrick came across to join him. 'José looked a bit off-colour last time I saw him.'

'He's lying down, resting quietly, I believe,' Patrick said.

'I felt a bit strange myself, last night. When the ship heaved a couple of times I can tell you, I was glad I was in my bunk. I wouldn't have liked to have been on deck at the time.'

'Slept through it all. You ought to try crossing the Irish Sea in a storm. Now that is something to be reckoned with.'

'The Irish Sea,' Rossend said 'Ireland. Let's see if I've got it right. What you were talking about yesterday evening. I can see there are many similarities between the situation in Ireland and to ourselves in Catalonia.'

'Precisely. Large neighbour, who thinks he has a right to have control over you.'

'Yet you know what's best for your country, more so than the neighbour does.'

'Right again,' Patrick said.

'Let me see if I've remembered what you've been saying,' Rossend said and drummed his fingers on the ship's rail. 'The Easter Uprising was in 1916.'

'Yes, it was,' Patrick said. 'And it was put down by the British.'

'So, Ireland didn't gain independence then?'

'No, it didn't.'

'You mentioned Boland's Mill. You knew the mill? It was important?'

'Boland's Mill, in Dublin. It was important in the 1916 Uprising. I'd managed a section of it before I turned professional, though I wasn't there at the time. Later, I went back to see my old workmates and find out what had gone on.'

'You didn't live in Dublin then?'

'Went back to Dublin in the summer. When the season was over, it was time to go home to see my mammy. I did that every year.'

'So, tell me again what happened?'

'The mill was by the Dublin Grand Canal and this was not far from the river. So when the Easter Uprising began, the mill was important. It gave a measure of control over the waterways. There was always the possibility that a gunboat or two would be sent up the Liffey.'

'The Liffey?'

'The river Dublin stands on.'

'The Liffey, right. The River Liffey.'

'When the money didn't stretch through the summer, I'd work at Ford's. You know Ford's, the motor company?'

'Well,' Rossend said, 'I know of it. An American company. I've read about it in the newspapers. Lorries are made there.'

'And motor cars. So, when I'd got a bit of money I'd go back to Dublin for a visit. And when I'd worked in Ford's I learned to drive. I'd learned in the factory yard.'

'You can drive?' Rossend asked.

'Naturally I can,' Patrick said. 'And once I brought a car home to where we were … Well, that's another story. It's not important at the moment.'

'You drove home in a car? I'm impressed. Everyone must have been.'

'And because I could drive … well, let's say it was useful for moving certain supplies around the city.'

'Supplies?'

'The Uprising was put down, fifteen men were shot, not to mention another man a little later on. People who hadn't been too bothered before about the British, changed their minds. Then it was only a matter of time before something really big happened. After those executions, a lot of people were determined that Ireland should gain its independence.'

'I understand.'

'I learned a lot from my visit to Boland's Mill. I wanted to help in some small way.'

1. Patrick O'Connell during his time at Hull City.

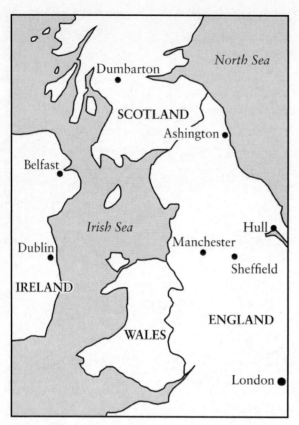

North Sea

Dumbarton

SCOTLAND

Ashington

Belfast

Irish Sea

Hull

Dublin

Manchester

Sheffield

IRELAND

ENGLAND

WALES

London

Left: 2. Map showing locations important to Patrick in the British Isles.

Below: 3. Map showing locations important to Patrick in Spain.

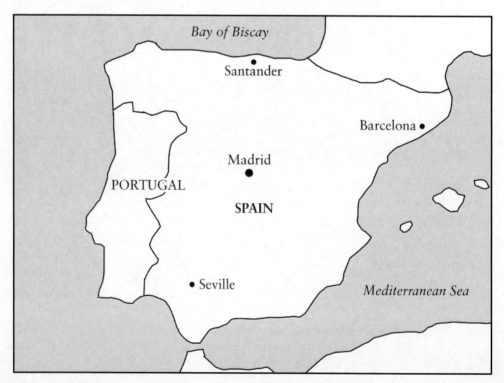

Bay of Biscay

Santander

Barcelona

Madrid

PORTUGAL

SPAIN

Seville

Mediterranean Sea

4. Sheffield Wednesday, 1909. Patrick is the player on the far right, second row.

5. A young Patrick, probably about twenty-two years old, in his early days with Sheffield Wednesday.

TO O'CONNELL, BEDAD!

To Paddy O'Connell – the top o' the mornin'!
Begorra, bedad, and bejabers, and that.
We're writin' an ode to ye; sure, and ye're worth it
You've talent, and Wednesday's the club to unearth it
And hasn't ould Oireland just givin ye a pat.

To-day ye've been footin' the leather v England,
'Gaint Simpson and Jefferis, and Freeman and Co.
Against our old fav'rites too, Holley and Mordue
And possibly plenty of work they'd afford you
But you'd have a say in the matter, we know.

Ould Oireland has niver defeated old England
(no blame to ye, 'Paddy', at all now, at all)
(Bad cess to these spalpeens on this side the water!)
But someday you'll get the odd trick, or you oughter
It won't be your fault if you don't? Pride must fall?

You made you debut (as friend 'Looker-On' tells us)
For Wednesday at Blackburn three seasons ago.
Began as a forward, a would-be goal getter;
Then tried the half-berth, and, all know it, did better,
Succeeded another "Pat" Connell, you know

Now (whisper it) Wednesday's going strong for the summit!
You're proud of your team tho' you mayn't be a 'Tyke'.
To-day you've been showing you're handy and natty;
(And maybe a far better 'feeder' than 'Fatty')
And Wednesday have proved you're the 'pat'-tern they like!

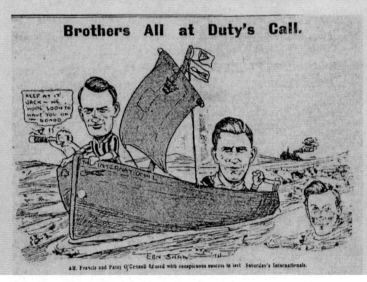

Brothers All at Duty's Call.

6. 'To O'Connell, Bedad!'

7. A group photo from Spain celebrating Real Betis winning the League in 1935, for which Patrick is remembered to this day. He is on the far left in the back row.

8. A portrait of Patrick with shirt and tie, among the very few possessions remaining with him at the time of his death.

9. The end of Patrick's career in the early 1950s, when he was rarely seen without his trilby. An old player told Sue that he wore it to hide his baldness.

'What did you do?'

'Unarmed people can't do much when they're fighting an empire.'

'You ran guns?'

'Never asked. Better that way'

'I'm sure you are right.'

'So, if I was stopped by any of the military patrols, I could honesty say I didn't know what was in the lorry, all I was doing was my job and that job was driving the lorry.'

'Clever strategy.'

'One of the footballers, he went on to great things in the new Irish Government, Minister of Posts and something. We all knew each other, put it that way.'

'The footballers?'

'Yes. We were a tight little group of footballers in Dublin, we'd all known each other for years, often since we'd been children. Dublin isn't a big place. So it was.'

'And what did that mean?'

'It was useful to have men who could drive, for whatever purpose was needed at the time.'

'When did Ireland gain independence, then. Did you say 1920?'

'No, the Irish Free State was founded in 1921.'

'But that wasn't all the island of Ireland, was it?'

'No, it wasn't. The British have kept a bit for themselves. Up there in the north.'

'That's what confuses me.'

'Confuses a lot of people.'

'Nearly lost it there,' Patrick said, as he grabbed his hat as the wind nearly took it off his head. 'The breeze is still a bit stiff.'

Rossend agreed. 'What do you think is going to happen?' he asked.

'In Catalonia? Who knows.'

'Do you think the Nationalists will get control?'

'Of course they won't,' Patrick said. 'Don't forget the Nationalists are fighting against a democratically elected government.'

'That doesn't seem to count for much these days.'

Rossend studied the horizon again.

'Is that Cuba?'

Patrick followed his gaze.

'I believe you're right,' he said. 'Listen to the lads. You can hear them. *Tierra a la vista*. Land ahoy. That must be Cuba.'

'We're nearly there,' Rossend said. 'The great adventure begins.'

Patrick's Letter from off the Coast of Cuba
to Ellie in Barcelona
June 1937

My Dearest Ellie

In a short time we arrive at La Havana, Cuba. I am taking this opportunity to send a letter to you, to let you know I am well and have arrived here safely across the Atlantic Ocean.

We have sailed along the coast for sometime and the team is on deck awaiting our arrival at the main port and capital. We are to spend a day here putting down and taking up passengers, then we sail to Veracruz and begin our journey in Mexico.

It was a great surprise to me that when we were in Paris as I met with some friends of mine from the world of football. The Irish national team were in the city and it was great to meet up with people I have not seen for an age.

I trust that you are well and taking the cod liver oil. I know you don't like it, though at the moment it is better you do take it. I also trust the Red Cross is not working you too hard. If everything gets too difficult do not forget the ships are waiting to take you and many others out of that terrible situation you are all enduring. In your present condition you will have priority. Don't forget this.

On our arrival in Mexico, I will write again.

Your loving husband,

Patrick.

Patrick's Story
Havana
June 1937

'You buy. You buy.' The little boy trotted along at the side of the group of men. 'You buy,' he chanted. 'Good deal.' The child opened the wooden box and showed a dozen cigars. 'Good bargain. Made by hand.'

Some of the men stopped to inspect the goods, others continued their leisurely walk along the sea front.

'I'm famished,' said Iborra. 'Got any money anyone? I've got to eat. I'm so hungry.' Two or three of the men followed him into a side street.

'You are Spanish?'

A man stood at the open door of a restaurant. 'Come in. Come in. You are Spanish?' He beckoned to the group of men. 'Come in. I was born and raised in Malaga. Come and eat here, please.'

The men followed him in to the dark, narrow room.

'Dolores.' The manager of the restaurant called to a shadowy figure at the back of the restaurant. 'We have visitors. From Spain.'

He turned to the group of men once again.

'How many of you are there? Six? Seven? You are all Spanish?' The words tumbled over each other and he greeted the men like old friends, shaking their hands, as he guided them to a table.

'Dolores,' he called. 'Quick. Quick. Get the soup ready for these men. Quick.' The man rushed around issuing orders to his wife and to the three or four children who had appeared from nowhere.

'Are you here for long?' the man asked. 'Will you be staying for long?'

'Sail this evening,' said one of the men. 'We're on our way to Mexico. Footballers. We're footballers.'

'I knew it,' said the manager of the restaurant. 'I knew it. Didn't I say. Dolores?' and he turned again towards the figure behind the counter. 'Didn't I say that these were no ordinary men. Footballers.'

His wife nodded and continued to ladle soup into the bowls. The man served the food, setting each bowl down with care. 'Black bean,' he said. 'Cuban black bean soup. You'll like it, especially the way my wife prepares it. It's good, very good. *¡Que aprovechen!*' He beamed at the men.

'Black bean,' said one of the men. 'Thank God, it's not chickpea. If I never see another chickpea for as long as I live that will be soon enough for me.' Then he dunked a large piece of bread into the bowl and caught the drips of soup in his mouth.

The children arranged themselves behind the chairs of the footballers. From time to time one or other of them would dart off to get more bread.

'Are you going to play a match here?' the eldest boy asked. 'Where are you going to play? Please, we'd like very much to watch.'

'Pester. Pester,' his father said. 'Can't you see these gentlemen are eating?' He stopped and looked around the table at the seated men. He gave a nervous laugh. 'That these *comrades* are eating.'

'Comrades, gentlemen. It's all the same to us,' said one of the players, taking up another spoonful of soup, 'We're footballers. Comrades. Gentlemen. We don't mind. It's all the same.'

Manager O'Connell held up his hand to quieten the conversation.

'Tell us your name,' he said to the eldest boy.

'Miguel.'

'Well, Miguel, I tell you what, if you raise a team by six o'clock this evening, you can play us. You can be the Captain and if you can get a team together by six o'clock, then you and your team can play us and then you'll be able to say that you have captained a team that played against FC Barcelona. How about that?'

The boy nodded.

'Down where the *Mexique* is moored. All right? At the harbour. You get a team together and we'll have a match. Six o'clock this evening. Agreed?'

'You like Cuban rice?' the manager of the restaurant interrupted. 'It's good, very good. A fried egg for everyone? Two fried eggs, however many fried eggs you want. Just tell me.'

'Fried eggs,' said Ventolrà. 'I'd forgotten that they ever existed.' Then he began forking great heaps of Cuban rice into his mouth.

When the last of the men put down his coffee cup, the wife of the restaurant manager came out from behind the counter. 'Please excuse me, señores,' she said, opening and closing her hands, 'but what is happening in the south? I have to ask. All my family, my parents, my brothers and sisters, they all live in Seville. What's happening there?'

The manager of the restaurant put his hand on his wife's arm. 'All my wife's family live in Seville. We haven't had a letter in more than a year.'

'We hear such terrible things,' the woman continued. 'My family ...'

'But we don't know what is happening. Just rumours and more rumours. It's ... and Dolores wanted to ask whether you knew anything of what's going on in Seville.'

'None of us are from the south,' one of the men said. 'We don't know, but Patrick here,' and he pointed to the manager, 'he used to live in Seville, didn't you Patrick?'

Patrick nodded, 'but that was when things were different, before all this started.'

One of the younger men interrupted. 'They can't win,' he said. 'They can't. We must win. We must. We have to.'

'Good. Good,' said the manager of the restaurant. 'That's good and now, who wants more coffee?'

'Yes,' said his wife. 'More coffee? Please. We don't want you to think that we don't know how to look after our customers here in La Havana. More coffee?'

The men left the restaurant. The young boy ran after them.

'I get my team,' he said. 'You no forget?'

'Forget?' Patrick said. 'How could we do that? No, you get your team and meet us down at the harbour and we'll play you. But you'll have to give us a good game, won't you?'

The boy nodded in agreement. Patrick turned and lifted his hat to the manager of the restaurant and his family. 'It'll be alright,' he said and walked in to the shadow of the narrow street to escape the heat of the Cuban afternoon.

Patrick's Story
The Gulf of Mexico
June 1937

A group of passengers stood watching the footballers.

'And three and four and stop.'

The players rested.

'Exercise, sea air and good food. You'll be in great form. No team will be better. Right. I want you back here as agreed for the afternoon training session.'

Some of the spectators wandered off. Most of the team followed. Iborra stayed for a moment.

'We were always taught at school about the Conquistadores. How they sailed from Spain and crossed the ocean sea. I never thought that I'd get to see Mexico for myself.'

'None of us expected it. Take it as a grand adventure.'

'They were brave men, those Conquistadores. They might have sailed to the edge of the world and fallen off.'

'They were brave men, indeed.'

'And they went back to Spain and told everyone what they had found.'

'They did, that they did. But I think that you are leading somewhere, not to a review of the history lessons from your days at the school?'

The young man sat down on the deck and leaned over to tie his shoelaces. 'Will we get back to Spain?' he asked.

'We're only just setting off, now. We left France four or five days ago. Not homesick already, are you?'

'It's not that. The west of Spain is going to fall in a couple of weeks, possibly a couple of days. It might have fallen already for all we know, here in the middle of the Atlantic Ocean.'

'A country divided is never a good thing.' Patrick said.

'Some of the team were talking about a negotiated peace. What do you think?'

'I doubt it.'

'And us?'

'The future is a dangerous thing. Don't look into it too closely. It is not always that you see what you want to see. We're Ambassadors for Sport and don't forget it.'

'For sport, I know.'

'Keep that in mind. We've been given a task and it is for us to complete it.'

'I suppose so. You're right.'

'You've got a grand opportunity. You're a young man. See the world and enjoy it.'

The player turned his attention back to his shoes and tied the other lace. 'Is that why you came to Spain? Please excuse my curiosity. I didn't mean to be impertinent.'

'It's a long story, worth the telling but not at present. Back here at five o'clock.'

'Manager.' Iborra regarded his shoelaces with satisfaction. 'Five o'clock, precisely. So British.'

Patrick looked at the young man.

'British,' he said. 'No. What's that got to do with it. And where's Ventolrà? I haven't seen him all day and he's missed training.'

'Seasick,' said Iborra. 'Can't raise his head from the pillow.'

'He ought to try crossing the Irish Sea in an autumn gale.' Patrick paused for a moment. 'Here. On deck. Five o'clock and don't forget.'

Patrick's Letter from the Port of Havana
to His Brother Larry in London
June 1937

Dear Larry

Didn't we have the greatest game of football in Havana? Just this very afternoon, not half an hour ago, when we all finished in triumph.

We played a ragamuffin team. The captain was a young lad we met today when we ate at his father's restaurant and his players were cousins and neighbours and a stray man or two the team picked up on its way to the harbour to come to challenge us. The second half of the match was shorter than the first half, as the crew were about to cast off without the team and we were not sure whether we were winning or losing, but they gave us a good game and that's all there is to that.

Now we are sailing for Mexico, to land in Veracruz and we'll see what awaits us. A great welcome and plenty to eat, if the stories that reach us are true.

The ship is very fine and comfortable, especially after the privations we have suffered over the past few months and years. When the ship has left us in Mexico, it will sail on to New York and then return to Europe and so there is every possibility that you will receive this letter.

The lads, who I am travelling with, are a wondrous lot. Some have scarcely been away from home before and are missing their wives and sweethearts already. Others are taken up with the adventure of it all. They take their responsibilities with great strength and courage. They are the Ambassadors of the Republic and of the Catalans. They will show the world what FC Barcelona can do, even in these times of great trouble.

We took the train for France from Barcelona. It is generally known here that the Nationalists have ships that patrol up and down the Mediterranean coast. They take pot shots at the trains as they travel between Barcelona and the frontier, but once we crossed the border the lights were turned on again and there was a holiday mood. Everyone was laughing and joking and asking where the team was going.

We stayed a while in Paris before setting off for the rest of our journey. News spreads like wild fire and we found that the Irish national team was in the city. I went over to the hotel where the team was staying, to introduce myself and I knew every last one of them – even down to the news reporter who travelled with the team, as one of his brothers used to play for Bohemians. You'll remember him. He worked at Boland's when I got to work there. It was a great reunion with them all and if you want the details go up to Kilburn and buy yourself a newspaper, because a fine piece will be printed on the happenings of the day – the day when we all met by chance in Paris and how it is that I am the Manager of the great FC Barcelona and that we are on our way to Mexico.

There is something I must say to you. If life gets too difficult in Barcelona, Ellie has promised me she will leave and that we will meet up again in Ireland. I ask that you help her on her way, if she passes through London.

Ellie still has her British passport and we have learned she will have the possibility of securing a place on one of the British ships. These ships come into the port of Barcelona to help the British fleeing this war. When these people, these poor exiles, get back to London they get collected from Victoria Station. From there they are taken to a place of refuge, a boarding house or such, that has been set up by the Spanish Emergency Committee. It is close to the station. This is where Ellie will go if she has to leave in a hurry. Once in London it would be easy for her to go over to Argyle Street and meet up with you. I know she can depend on you for help whatever happens.

It almost slipped my mind. You'll have to treat me with more respect next time we meet as I'm now an Honorary Consul for the Spanish Republic. This has been bestowed on me by the Government, as we undertake the tour as Ambassadors for Sports. In future, I expect you to write Hon. Consul after my name, on envelopes etc. as befits my newly acquired status.

I must finish this letter. The night is warm, the skies are clear and somewhere off our port side is Mexico. The lads tell me that they have seen dolphins and possibly a shark. I'm going to check for myself. Me, I'm rather taken by the flying fish.

I will leave you for the moment.

Your brother.

Patrick.

I will try to let you know of our travelling plans though they change day by day, in the hope that you will be able to join us in Paris on our return journey. Then, we may both go to the Paris Opera together.

We spent a day in Cuba so I am writing to you as the mail service is better on this side of the Atlantic than that from Barcelona. I am not certain that you will have received my previous letters.

Patrick's Letter from the Gulf of Mexico
to Ellie in Barcelona
June 1937

My Dearest Ellie

As I write this, the ship is casting off from La Havana and the coast of Mexico is only hours away.

I think about you frequently, especially at this time and almost gave away our secret when we were eating in a restaurant. It was run by a husband and wife from Spain. They were helped out by their children who ran around serving us bread and a dozen other things. It made me think about family life and what is waiting for us in the years to come.

This letter gives me the opportunity to let you know that I am safe and well. The journey to the French border was largely free of events, if a little dark. We had to travel through the night with all the lights of the train turned off, so that we did not give a ready target to any patrolling Nationalist ships. A slight difficulty but no more.

From the frontier we travelled to Paris. Some of the French passengers were very encouraging, assuring us the Republic will win, though one fellow did say to me that 'We are next', meaning I suspect that fascism will take over in France, once it has succeeded in Spain. He was a pleasant man and wanted to talk throughout the journey, though his command of Spanish was limited and, as you know, my knowledge of French none existent. He told me his nephew wanted to go to Spain to fight for the Republic but as he was only fifteen years old so far, has been prevented by his parents from slipping off over the frontier, to join the International Brigades.

How I wish that you had been with me to share the time together in Paris. It seems even more beautiful than on my previous visits, a magnificent city;

wide boulevards, exceptional buildings and free of war. Though our time there was brief, we all befitted from it. Then we continued to the coast, to board our ship.

It is a fine ship and many of the passengers are from Spain. Amongst the passengers are many children, Catalans and Basques mainly. They are all desperately sad to be leaving their families and their homes. The boys and many of the girls vow to return once they are old enough. They know that their fathers and older brothers are fighting for the Republic and some of them have died for that cause. They know that they are being sent to Mexico for safety, but they say they will go back as soon as they are able.

One of the children, Iñaki by name, a boy from the Basque region, has befriended me. He continues to follow me about the ship day and night and watches our training sessions but he never speaks. One of the nurses travelling with the children tells me that he saw his mother killed in a bombing raid and that his father is feared dead.

The boy will be cared for in Mexico at a children's village, along with many of the other children who do not have family there. The village has been specially built by the Mexican government, as a gesture in the fight against fascism. The nurses tell me that the village is a very modern place and has everything to help the children forget the pain they have suffered. They are given medical treatment. There are classrooms and sports grounds, a truly wonderful place for them to recover from the grief and fear they have suffered.

On the way to Mexico, we put in for a day or so to the port of La Havana, Cuba. We had time to go ashore and some of us took a walk through the city. We stopped to eat at a small restaurant that was run by a husband and wife, who happened to be from Spain. The wife asked us again and again if we had any news from the South. She was very distressed and her husband told us that she has family living in Seville and has not heard from them for many months. Of course, she fears the worst. As we left the wife gave us some biscuits and cakes for the children on board ship.

When we gave the cakes to the children, Iñaki said, '*Eskerrik asko,*' and the other children interpreted for us. Apparently, it means 'thank you' in the Basque language and the other children said that Iñaki must be getting better, because this is the first time they have heard him speak.

We do fitness exercises on deck each morning and are joined by some of the passengers, adults and children. We are well known now on board ship and many of our fellow travellers promise to come to watch us play when we all get to Mexico City.

The team is anxious to arrive in Mexico. They take it in turn to stand on deck and watch for land. Iborra says to me that I am not to tell you about the food, as you will continue to suffer the shortages of rationing, whilst we here even on board ship, are able to eat our fill. The men say that Mexican food is unlike anything we have in Europe. They are obsessed by food. I am sure it is all some of the younger ones think about.

A shout has gone up. The coast of Mexico must be in sight. I will go to join the men.

These are difficult times. Take care of yourself as much as is possible.

Remember that I think of you always, especially now.

Your loving husband,

Patrick.

Voice of Mexico
Mexico City
8 June 1937

From Our Roving Sports Correspondent
Finally that magnificent team, the great FC Barcelona is here.

Yesterday the imposing ship the *Mexique*, sailed into the Port of Veracruz. On board were the FC Barcelona Team, their team manager and support staff.

These footballers have left behind a land ravaged by war. They have braved all in the name of Sport and International Brotherhood; a difficult and tiring journey by land and sea and what is more, they have been shot at and risked aerial bombardment too. Now they have arrived at the shores of our Great Nation.

That well-known businessman Miguel Mas Serrano, sent the invitation to the team. Before he emigrated to Mexico Señor Mas Serrano himself, used to play baseball at the FC Barcelona Sport Complex Polígano and he continues a keen supporter of his home football team to this day.

Our readers will be aware of the troubles faced by those living in war-torn Barcelona. Many of the supporters who follow the team are fighting Fascism and whilst they are battling with the rebels, FC Barcelona does not have the same extensive crowds to which it has become accustomed. This has caused certain financial constraints, which are not merited by the magnificent level of play offered by this great team.

FC Barcelona is here to show the Mexican people their impressive sporting skills and to offer us some superb entertainment as well.

The team will shortly begin the next stage of their journey, as they travel from Veracruz to Mexico City. Once there the men, under the direction of Manager and Trainer Mister Patrick O'Connell, will continue their gruelling training programme. The plan is to be back in form by the third week in June, by which time the team ought to be used to the altitude of our capital city.

FC Barcelona has undertaken to play a series of matches – six in all – with our First Division Clubs of América, Asturias, Atlante, España and two games with Necaxa.

The first match against América is scheduled for Sunday, 20th June 1937, in the España Park. Kick off is at 11:30 am, to allow the match to be concluded before the rains begin.

Let us give FC Barcelona our fraternal support, today and throughout their visit.

Look out for our exclusive interview with Manager Mr Patrick O'Connell, which will appear later in the week.

¡Viva México! ¡Viva la República! ¡Viva!

Patrick's Story
Mexico City
June 1937

'Come on. Pass, pass. Come on. Stop dreaming, will you?'

The player put in a brief surge of energy, kicked the ball and sank to his knees. Manager O'Connell walked over. 'We've got five days. Come on, you can do it.'

The player lay gasping, his arm over his face.

'Can't breathe … can't breathe … none of us can.' He rolled on to his side and lay still. 'We haven't had long enough … to get used to the air here … Oh God. I'm going to die …' He took a deep breath and groaned.

One of the other players ran his hand over his own face. 'Look,' he said. 'It's the second nosebleed I've had today.'

'Get away,' said another player. 'Lucky it's not a bullet wound.'

'Ten minute break,' said the manager. 'Ten minutes and no more. The rains will start in an hour.'

The men collapsed on to the pitch. Patrick sat down with them.

'Will you look at that,' he said. 'Did you ever think that you would live to see a volcano? Two of them, no less. A wonderful sight. Impressive, don't you think?' Some of the players turned to look. The volcanos rose out of the mist, plumes of cloud trailing from their summits. 'Will you look at that?'

'Are they going to erupt?' asked one of the men.

'Argh, no and even if they did, they wouldn't get to us here.'

'My grandmother says it's the end of the world.'

'She does, does she?'

'She says it's the end of the world. Wars … tempests … the anti-Christ has come.'

'In my father's village they've shot the priest and burned down the church.'

'About time too.'

'You've changed your opinions.'

'I didn't understand the ways of the world before.'

'And you do now?'

'Think what they've done here in Mexico. No churches. No priests. No ...'

Manager O'Connell interrupted. 'We are visitors here. We are here for the sport. Remember that.'

One of the players whistled a tune.

'That's our song,' said Iborra. 'The Mexicans have written a song for us. Listen.'

A couple of players joined in with the words.

'Someone was playing it outside the hotel this morning, over and over.' said Ventolrà. 'Guitar, violin and double base, standing, singing in the street, in front of the hotel and last night at the banquet ...' He stopped and looked around him.

Manager O'Connell threw down his cigarette and got up.

'And which banquet would that be? Can't breathe to play for the team, can't breathe to play for the Republic ... but can breathe to eat, drink and dance the night away. Banquets are supposed to be forbidden until the team is used to the altitude. You remember our agreement, don't you? Come on ... to your feet and I mean now.'

A groan went up from the men.

'You're a hard man, Manager.'

'Hey, Balmanya, pass me the ball.'

Patrick's Letter from Mexico City
to His Brother Larry in London
June 1937

Dear Larry

Rumours and counter-rumours concerning the Spanish Republic are sweeping through this city. So, in case the Nationalists have spread their false stories to London and you, yourself hear them – believe me when I tell you categorically, there is no guillotine in Barcelona. No guillotine and no communal grave in the main square, waiting for the bodies of those who have just lost their heads.

The Generalísimo's supporters repeat these base tales to indicate the behaviour of the Republicans is of the worst possible type and that appalling acts are committed, like those of the darkest days of the French Revolution.

Only yesterday our young physiotherapist Angel, was shown what was supposed to be a photograph of this guillotine. I can assure you that it does not exist and that this was merely a clever trick of the camera.

There are difficulties in the Republic certainly and there is also conflict between the groups on the political left but no, not one of us has seen a guillotine in the Plaza de Catalunya and I can state with no hesitation some of us would have noticed the tumbrels rolling past or recalled seeing the baskets of severed heads. This is a pure invention to besmirch the name of the Republic. Ask yourself who are the barbarians.

The first match of the tour has now been set for the 20th of this month and until then, we must divide our time between training and resting (the official programme) and being wined and dined (the unofficial programme). It is hard for me to confess this but I have given in to some of the demands of the social programme, which has proved to be very popular with the men.

From the day we arrived, those Mexicans who do not believe we are uncivilized barbarians – and there are many who do believe we are of the very lowest, due to the tales of the Nationalists – have fêted us, honouring the team as Ambassadors of the Republic and Ambassadors for Sport. Each evening we are invited to banquets and dinners and a dozen toasts are offered to the success of the Tour, to the enduring friendship between the Mexican people and the Spanish Republic and to the International Brotherhood of Sportsmen.

The Mexicans present us with such food as you have never seen nor tasted in Europe; food wrapped in small pancakes made of Indian corn, turkey cooked in spicy chocolate sauces, food baked in the enormous leaves of the banana plant. The team eats and tries to remember what it is that they have been served. They eat and enjoy themselves and I have to say, are catching the attention of many of the local señoritas.

You would like this place, Larry. It is a place you could enjoy – here in the city, there is what is termed the Bellas Artes Concert Hall, built of finest marble and offering world class opera performances and close by the Palace of Tiles, built for one of the Spanish Conquerors. It is a building of great beauty and culture.

There are motorcars and trolley buses on the streets, yet some of the Mexican people dress as their ancestors did 500 years ago and use strange words from a language never heard in Spain. The cinemas show the latest Hollywood productions, whilst the walls of the public buildings are painted with revolutionary slogans as I understand, you might expect to see in the Soviet Union. It is a truly remarkable country.

We sit here enjoying a beer in the courtyard of the Continental Hotel, as far above sea level as the highest peaks of the Alps and try to get used to breathing the thin air of this city in the mountains.

We arrived here expecting to stay two weeks or maybe three. Now it is almost certain that we will remain two months or maybe three.

Write to me here at the hotel.

Your brother,

Patrick.

PS – Something that will amuse you.

As honoured guests in this strange and wonderful country, we were taken to Xochimilco, a village a little beyond the city limits. Here, we found a veritable network of small canals running between what are known as 'floating gardens'. These so-called gardens supply the city with vegetables and flowers and we are told, have been used since before the Spanish Conquistadores arrived here.

It is something the locals try to persuade visitors that if they were to plant a stick in the ground, it would grow – not like those fields in Galway and Connemara where, after twenty years of careful plying with seaweed, a poor patch of pratties might be coaxed from the ground. These small fields yield two or even three crops a year. Imagine that if you can, the land is so fertile.

The locals travel between these fields in little gondola-like boats. These little boats are rented out on high days and holidays to visitors and pleasure seekers. This way we were treated to an excursion: the team, the entourage and our hosts, accompanied at a respectable distance by a boat loaded to sinking-point with a troupe of musicians plus violins, guitars, double bass, trumpets and I don't know what else, for us to enjoy the day singing awhile the Mexican songs. You would have been joining in the choruses in no time.

So our flotilla progressed slowly and somewhat unsteadily, along the waterways, until the thunderclouds heralded the daily downpour. We disembarked at a country restaurant to sample some of the local specialities. Here people do not eat bread such as you or I would recognise, but rather little flat cakes made of Indian corn. These snacks were urged upon us: pancakes, filling and a sauce that appeared to be made of tomato. Though the food was served at normal temperature, the effect was like biting into molten steel, 'The Mexican chilli – beware,' said our hosts, rocking with laughter, as we coughed and spluttered. Here the people will eat chilli peppers as a child in Ireland or England would eat sweets, yet to us Europeans, they are the very devil.

In good humour the lads have vowed they will not fall into this trap again and are planning to be very cautious in what they eat.

Voice of Mexico – Exclusive Interview
with FC Barcelona Manager Patrick O'Connell
June 1937

From our Roving Reporter

The Mexican People extend the hand of friendship to the great FC Barcelona and to the Team Manager, Mister Patrick O'Connell.

Newspaper Reporter: This is a historic moment. For the first time the renowned FC Barcelona is here in Mexico. The team is scheduled to play six matches with some of our best teams. How do you feel about this?

Manager Mr Patrick O'Connell: The Team and I are looking forward to the matches. We expect some strong competition, exciting games and fine challenges. It's very encouraging that so many spectators are turning out to watch our training sessions and there is so much interest in our progress.

Newspaper Reporter: We understand FC Barcelona has followed a training programme even during the voyage across the Atlantic Ocean. Are the men fully prepared for the games?

Manager Mr Patrick O'Connell: Even on board ship the FC Barcelona Team followed a daily training programme. It's taking the Team a little time to get used to the altitude here in Mexico City but they are young men and they are strong men. I am confident the players will overcome any difficulty in time for the first match, scheduled for Sunday, 20th June against El América and is to be played in one of the main parks.

Newspaper Reporter: Does the style of football differ from that the team is used to? How does European football contrast with football played here?

Manager Mr Patrick O'Connell: Over the past few days we have had the opportunity to watch some of your training sessions and we see you have some promising players, as we do in Europe. Our team has played in some difficult circumstances, so I feel the men will be able to adapt to what is demanded of them. I want to tell your readers 'We're ready! Good and ready!'

Newspaper Reporter: And after Mexico, where are you planning to go to next? We have heard this tour referred to as a 'World Tour'? How long do you expect to remain in Mexico?

Manager Mr Patrick O'Connell: The plan is to remain until we have completed the series of six matches, here in Mexico City. We have the possibility of an extra match in Orizaba, as we make our way back to the coast to continue our tour. From Mexico we sail to New York and there we will review the situation.

Newspaper Reporter: We understand you were a player before you became a manager. Would you tell our readers a little about your career as a professional footballer?

Manager Mr Patrick O'Connell: Indeed. Before I became a manager I was indeed a player. My career began in Dublin – my home town. I played for Liffey Wanderers and moved to Belfast for my first professional signing. Eventually, I was Captain of our National Team on various occasions between 1912 and 1914. I have had some success, most notably captaining the National team when we won the 'Triple Crown', that is the series of matches between Ireland, England, Scotland and Wales – this was before Irish Independence – for the first time in 1914. With the move to England I played for Sheffield Wednesday, Hull City and for Manchester United. I captained the Team in 1915 and beyond, through the Great War.

Newspaper Reporter: In Spain, what are conditions like in the Republic? Reports suggest life is very difficult there. We have been told that your train was subject to aerial bombardment as you and the team started out on your journey to Mexico.

Manager Mr Patrick O'Connell: As I am sure many of your readers are aware life in Barcelona and all Spain, is somewhat troubled at present. As people will know, there has been an uprising against the elected government. We are here to show the best the Republic has to offer in the World of Sport. We come as Ambassadors.

Newspaper Reporter: Finally, though of great importance: What is your opinion of Mexico and the Mexican people?

Manager Mr Patrick O'Connell: We have met with kindness at every turn. People have gone out of their way to take care of our welfare. We have one request however – can we have our luggage back? We haven't seen it since we arrived in Mexico City.

¡Viva México! ¡Viva FC Barcelona! ¡Viva!

Ellie's Letter from London
to Her Sister Mary in Ireland
July 1937

Mary, Mary

I've lost the baby. I'm so wretched and exhausted and hardly know how I arrived here in London.

The baby would have been a boy and I was so happy. I think Patrick would have been too – our own little son and now he is gone. What is worse is that Patrick doesn't know yet and of course, I can't get in contact with him and in any case, would not consider it would be right to tell him while he is away.

After all these years of marriage, it was the greatest of surprises and greatest of pleasures to discover that I was expecting. It was, of course, the worst of times for such joy and now this great happiness is lost and will never be again.

The staff at the Red Cross clinic persuaded Patrick it was better to send me away, out of all this trouble and war. Yet, if I had stayed I might not have lost the baby. Our little son, that never was. But all is confusion and turmoil in our magnificent city and it was decided that in my condition, it was best for me to go, whatever my intentions had been to begin with. I had to leave Patrick as he set off with the team to Mexico. It broke my heart to see him go.

Dear God, let it be Patrick gets to safety. Our dear little son is no more and I feel so wretched. The thought I might have lost both of them fills me with such pain. I had so much. I had too much and now it is all gone. Everything was given to us both and now it is taken away.

Pray for me in this time of desolation.

Your loving sister,

Ellie.

Please write to me soon, by return of post if it is possible. I am staying here in London, in Wimbledon with the family, and will stay here until I have the strength to travel back to Ireland. When I arrived it was too painful for me to go to Larry's hotel. My spirit would die if Patrick has not managed to get away from the war and has not survived. I couldn't bare to lose both of them in such a short time. My heart would break.

When my health is a little restored I will go back into the city and check the lists of refugees at the rooms of the Spanish Emergency Committee. I will hope and pray Patrick's name is among those who have managed to make it back to London.

Patrick's Letter from Mexico City
to His Brother Larry in London
August 1937

Dear Larry

The final tally in Mexico City is a respectable 6 out of 9 wins to us. However, by the end of the series the Mexicans had employed a clever weapon, we none of us had expected and we lost the last two matches held in Mexico City.

We have got used to the rarified air up here but what we didn't expect was that the Mexicans would feed us and fête us at every turn, inviting us to banquets and parties. Every day is gala day. We are, I believe, like Hollywood stars here. When we first arrived we resisted the pressure to attend these events, though when we were told we were insulting the Mexican people by doing this, we accepted their invitations. So many good meals and the team loses the edge in a game. To cap it all, one of the men is deeply in love and I doubt that we will get him as far as New York. In total, this all serves to undermine a serious regime of early nights and rigorous training.

After the years of deprivation and scarcity I must say, it is difficult to keep the lads away from a little fun and a few bright lights. They can hold their heads high and overall have behaved in a most exemplary manner, sufficient for their gentlemanly behaviour and general good conduct to be remarked upon in the national press.

When we first arrived here there were those who sought to discredit us at every turn, as a band of ruffians and unruly Reds. The team has earned the respect of all – even some of the most diehard supporters of the Nationalists. The lads are without doubt, Ambassadors of Sport of the finest sort.

There are plans afoot that we will play one final game before we leave Mexico and sail from Veracruz for New York. It is the intention to stop for a night or two, at the town of Orizaba, mid-point on our return journey to the coast. It is a brewery town and as such, there is a certain appeal for the men beyond the possibility of playing an extra game of football.

It has been necessary to start the entire series of matches here in Mexico, with kick-off in the mornings, as it is the rainy season. By mid-day the clouds are building, by early afternoon the thunder starts to roll and then the rain begins with the massive storms playing out against the surrounding volcanos. Altogether this is an impressive sight, enough to make one realise how very far Mexico is from Europe. The noise is intense, lightening cracks across the sky, the streets run with water and then everything clears, only to repeat the entire process the following day.

It would be good to meet up with you in Paris on our return journey. Is there any possibility of you bringing another suit? Our physiotherapist Angel, managed to get his stolen. It is his intension to come along to the Paris Opera with us, where he says shorts and football boots are not appropriate apparel.

Due to the foresight of Rossend Calvert, the money (raised by this series of matches here, in Mexico) was safe when the robbery took place. Had that money been taken, it would have been a terrible blow, but no, we still have the cash and will save the team yet.

And so to the United States of America and I'm bound to say I find the idea appealing. It is a place we hear so much of and I never expected to see.

Write to me at our hotel in New York.

Your brother,

Patrick.

I've enclosed the address of our hotel.

Patrick's Letter from New York
to Ellie in London
September 1937

My Dearest Ellie

The Tour is coming to an end and soon most of us will be shipping back to Europe. We leave with mixed feelings. Joy at seeing family and friends once more, but pain at what is happening at this time in Spain and beyond. It does not need to be said how much I am looking forward to seeing you again and trust that I might arrive to find that I am returning to the two of you.

We arrived here in triumph, were written about in the press and put on display as Europe's finest. Now the Generalísimo graces the front cover of the news magazines and we are relegated to yesterday. We have raised a quantity of money, not much but enough to fight another day. Our supporters have been very generous.

In New York I've done much walking, to get a feel for the character of the city. I strolled along Fifth Avenue, with you in mind. You would have enjoyed it. There are shops with all the latest fashions and the women look so elegant, though I do understand it might be some time before the latest fashions fit you once more.

Larry intends to meet up with me when we get back to France and has great plans for us to go to the Paris Opera. When the doorman sees my clothes, I fully doubt he will let me in, but rather expel me as a vagabond and tramp. Larry writes that he will do what he can to bring an old jacket he has to spare. This is in addition to the suit he has been asked to bring for our young physiotherapist, who managed to get his stolen.

I will write again soon. Keep yourself and the little one safe.

Your loving husband,

Patrick.

Young Ventolrà, is to stay and settle in Mexico and marry his lady love, the niece of President Lázaro Cardenas himself, no less.

Patrick's Story
New York
September 1937

It put me to wondering
How many of my compatriots have arrived here.
Go on. Stand here, beside me.

Look across the harbour.

See what they saw. See what they see.

Spectacular, isn't it?

Fairly takes the breath away.

They've arrived here for a hundred years, full of expectation regarding the new life they are about to begin.

How many of my compatriots have gasped in amazement at the buildings.

And once they have got ashore been amazed at all the rushing traffic, more vehicles in one street than they have seen in their entire lives before this.

What a country they were about to enter.

How many of my compatriots have been lost for words as they looked around, lost in wonder at what they saw.

Been dumbfounded by this New World.

Tens of thousands have poured into this port from Ireland, no, hundreds of thousands.

Would anyone notice one more?

One more Irishman, disappearing into the crowd.

Starting again.

I've done it before.

Started a new life in Spain.

Why not do the same again here in the USA?

There must be room for one more person.

If not in New York, there must be plenty of opportunity between here and the next ocean.

The frontier in Spain has swept on since we sailed for Mexico. Bilbao has fallen.

The Nationalist armies are at the doors of the fair, beautiful city of Barcelona.

The Republic and all its hopes and dreams are doomed.

Where Spain is today, the rest of Europe will be tomorrow.

Tearing itself apart.

Why would any sane man go back to that maelstrom?

Would anyone notice one more Irishman?

Lost amongst the millions of arrivals here in a country free from war.

It is a thought that comes to my mind. Standing here at the point of entry to the New World.

Tempting, especially when standing here on the banks of this mighty river with a beautiful park surrounding me.

But after reflection I think not.

I began this as Tour Manager. I will continue to the end as Tour Manager.

There's a certain responsibility with the job.

The money we raised must be safely banked in France.

All $12,500 US dollars of it.

To await whatever purpose is decided for it.

When all this is over, when things have settled down.

It'll be required.

Take away the club and you take away hope for the ordinary working man. He has precious little and will have even less when the Generalísimo takes full control.

Let me finish this cigarette.

Complete what I set out to do.

That's essential.

Something will turn up.

And my darling Ellie waits for me with my new baby son or daughter. It is strange to become a father again, thirty years after the first occasion. It would indeed be strange if the child is a boy and we call him 'Patrick'.

Patrick's Letter from New York
to His Brother Larry in London
October 1937

Dear Larry

We're here. We've arrived in New York. I feel like a child with the excitement of it all. Everything you have ever read about this city, seen at the cinema and have sung about in the songs, I must say it's true. Think like this and then add all the superlatives you have ever known and you will have a clearer idea of what this city is like. If anything, it is faster, larger, grander than we have been told.

The people here never sleep. The streets are thronged in the early hours of the morning, the good citizens on their way to I-can't-imagine-where. Traffic rumbling along wide avenues decorated with huge advertisement and these made up of a hundred thousand lights, dancing and sparkling across entire buildings and this only hints at what is here.

We sailed in to the port, with all the team on deck, eager to see the first sight of New York. We looked out and saw a skyline and what a skyline – think of London only fifty stories higher, no, one hundred stories higher, great skyscrapers wherever you care to look. We sailed past the Statue of Liberty, torch held aloft and the lads were standing on deck with their mouths agape. We moored up at the piers and to everyone's amazement in no time at all we were on Broadway, the Broadway of a thousand American films.

The men behave like children, all wanting to explore. This does however, bring its own particular problems, as we are now in the English-speaking world and I am their guide and protector. Times without number they ask, 'What does that mean?', 'How do you say?', 'What's happening?' And they scurry along, as if afraid of being left on their own, in a world they are having some difficulty in comprehending. Happy only when their interpreter and translator is close at hand, to shepherd them and help them out of difficulties when they cannot speak for themselves.

Keen to venture forth despite many trepidation, they want me to walk about the place all day long as well as half the night. I accompanied them as far as Times Square. What a spectacular sight of flashing lights that is, with illuminated advertisements and people rushing everywhere, with taxis, buses and even private motor cars.

There, miracle to behold, a group of young people were singing songs in Spanish. These young people term themselves 'No Pasarán', the expression used by the Spanish Republicans to vouch the Nationalist armies will not advance another step. Immediately, these young people discovered we were members of a football team from the Republic, FC Barcelona no less, and we were greeted as heroes. It was as if we had just returned from the front line and were personally responsible for holding the forces of fascism at bay. We proved to be their very own living specimens from the war.

I forget myself. Larry, You must excuse me the length of this letter but again we are living through such experiences that few others will ever have. It is impossible for me to stop writing so much to you.

I go back to these young people. These singers are all involved in raising funds for the Republic, for ambulances and medical supplies and for milk for the children caught in this terrible Spanish War. They have fathers, brothers, husbands or fiancés involved in the fighting. One singer had, I believe, recently returned from the Abraham Lincoln Regiment of the International Brigades. He was severely wounded at the battle of Jarama and was still recovering from his injuries. The lad could scarcely stand but still insisted in doing what he could to help. Altogether, we were treated very warmly and in reply, some of the lads joined in the singing and general collecting of money.

Now it appears some of the team will accompany the singers and go to Spanish Harlem, where it is hoped they will feel more at home. It is also their intension to do what is possible to rally more support for our matches. This will give me an opportunity to abandon my charges for an hour or two. It would not suit me to go along as nurse-maid with the entire team. I have a mind to visit Radio City and the Empire State Building, as I am told they are particularly impressive places to see.

It almost slipped my mind to tell you, though how I could do this I do not know. The team and I shipped here with some two hundred women. What do you think of that? It appears the Hispanic people supply the USA with labour in much the same way as the Irish supply the English. The two hundred are destined to work in domestic service, though all seemed to believe they are going to make their fortunes in New York and the streets would be paved with gold. Together, we sailed along the Gulf Coast and the Eastern Seaboard, a team of young footballers and a bevy of beauties, trapped together in the heat of a late summer. It was an experience of no little interest.

There was many a broken heart and many a tearful farewell when we reached our destination. In the meantime, it became common practice to knock loudly on the cabin door and wait, affording utmost discretion and no hurried entry, when one called by to speak to a member of the team about a trifling matter of match organisation or strategy.

We set sail on this voyage with such hope. We come from the Spanish Republic as Ambassadors for Sport. And what now? The future bodes ill for us all. Some of the lads were distressed to come across a recent issue of '*Time*,' an illustrated news magazine. On the front cover was a photograph of the Generalísimo Franco, in all his finery, looking as if he would be King. None of us have the heart to think about the morrow. We must continue day by day.

The men are coming back. We have an early start for training tomorrow.

I am as ever,

Your brother,

Patrick.

A schedule of games has been arranged here in New York, though there is some squabbling over who gets paid what, for which match. It has to be said that in the United States there is not the same level of enthusiasm for football or 'soccer' as it is termed here, as is found with the Europeans and the Mexicans. To balance this, our first match was kicked off by Ambassador Fernando de los Ríos, representative of the Spanish Republic to the United States of America. The Ambassador was most anxious to get news from home, yet managed to retain a quiet dignity throughout.

Patrick's Letter from Paris
to His Brother Larry in London
October 1937

Dear Larry

Once more we are back in France, our 'World Tour' over and completed, after matches in but two countries. The news from Spain is even worse than expected, whilst the situation in France appears to be confused.

You may congratulate us however, as we did achieve one of our main objectives – the great FC Barcelona will fight another day.

The magnificent sum of $12,500 (US dollars) is at present in the hotel safe and first thing tomorrow will be paid into a Paris bank. This is the amount of our takings from the matches in Mexico and the USA, along with donations from well-wishers. So, the future of the Club is assured whatever troubles are thrown at it. Who knows, this money may well lay the foundations for the distant future of the Club.

As the Tour reaches its final stage, only four or five of us will return to Barcelona. Two or three of the men have already settled in Mexico, the others are preoccupied with trying to obtain jobs and visas to enable them to remain in France.

When you come over to Paris you won't forget to bring with you a suit for young Angel and an extra jacket for me? Angel, the young physiotherapist and I will not be admitted to any respectable building – the Opera House or otherwise – given the sorry state our clothes are in.

I will meet you off the Boat Train as previously agreed.

Your brother,

Patrick.

1938

The Dazzler's Story
Manchester
April 1938

In the corner of the room the little boy squatted down and offered one of the wooden building blocks to his sister. She pushed it away and gave her attention to a rag doll.

'Have you got a change of clothes for him?'

'Enough to last him through the week.'

The little boy picked up another building block and ran backwards and forward across the room. On each trip he brought a wooden brick for inspection. He dropped it on to his mother's knee, then ran back to fetch the next one.

'Pyjamas?' said Nell. 'Have you put in any pyjamas for him?'

'With the other clothes and his toothbrush.'

One of the wooden blocks rolled off the young woman's knee. She caught it and handed it back to the child.

'He's only just three years old,' she said. 'I can't bear to be without you, can I Mickie Dazzler?'

The little boy came back with another building block.

'The child can't go on like that. He needs to see a specialist. Think of him.'

There was a wail from the baby. Nancy Manuel took the handle of the pram and rocked it back and forth.

'There, there,' she said. 'Don't cry. Please don't cry. You'll only set the others off.'

She looked across to the little girl crawling on the floor. 'Look what you big brother has got for you. Give her the dolly. Go on, pick it up for your sister. That's a good boy.'

The little girl took the doll from her brother and cradled it in her arms.

'It's the expense. We hadn't expected it,' said Nancy Manuel. She held out another of the wooden bricks to the little boy. 'We're trying to get ourselves sorted, we really are.'

Nell looked around the room. 'I can see that,' she said.

'Where's Patrick? I can't wait much longer.'

'Seeing the foreman. About the new job. He said he'll try to get back before you leave.'

One of the building blocks fell to the floor. Nancy Manuel tried to pick it up. 'We're grateful,' she said. 'We really are, for what you and Gran are doing for the Dazzler. I'd take him to the specialist's myself only ...' She trailed off in to silence.

'It's three bus rides,' Nell said. 'And besides with the Dazzler, a toddler and the pram, I hardly think it's a practical suggestion. Mother wants to take him to the hospital. And the sooner the better. All you have to do is look at his skin. That eczema is terrible. The child is suffering. It's for the best at present, if he comes to live with us.'

Nell reached out to the little boy. 'Come on. Let's go back to your Gran before it gets dark.'

The little boy went on playing with the wooden bricks. With great effort, Nancy got to her feet. 'His coat.'

Nell picked it up from the back of the chair and held it for the child to put on. 'Let's get your coat. Come on, the Dazzler. We've got to go and see your Gran. We can't wait forever for your daddy to get home.'

The little boy ran round the table to his mother and stretched up his arms to her. 'Up,' he said. 'Up. I want up.'

His mother turned towards him. 'Not now,' she said. 'I can't. Not now.'

Ellie's Letter from London
to Her Sister Mary in Ireland
May 1938

Dear Mary

My dear, dear Mary, I was so happy to receive your letter this morning that I'm replying immediately.

I still feel wretched, but I try to progress a little. Sometimes, I think about my great loss and sometimes I try not to remember it at all, as the pain is too much to bare.

Is it possible that I have lost Patrick as well? I pray for him every day and when I have the strength, go to Victoria Station to the rooms of the Emergency Committee. The helpers are so good. They check and re-check the lists of new arrivals from Spain, to see if Patrick's name is there, though I have no news of him. I fear the worst, yet hope and pray for the best.

Here, in London the talk is of war. Everyone expects England to go to war, with Herr Hitler and his Nazis party. Already there are plans to put sand bags around the main buildings and many of the windows are covered with tape to stop them shattering. These measures are intended to reduce the amount of damage bombing would cause. I have my doubts though, after what I have seen in Barcelona but I hope they are effective. I have experienced the damage bombing can do. It is a terrible thing. I have escaped one war, to be plunged into another.

People are already talking of shortages and rationing but they do not nearly understand these things. Shortages are when there is no bread in the entire city and people feast on cats and dogs. Do not be shocked – I have seen it and most certainly have done it, too.

As soon as I was able I left the boarding house run by the Emergency Committee and travelled out to West London to meet up with the family. It was a great joy to see them all. They are however, talking of returning to Ireland, for the sake of the children. It was a great relief to me they hadn't already left.

I must tell you that our niece was there. She is quite the grown up young lady now and attends the local convent. She walked down to the market with me and was very entertained and fascinated, when I remarked time and time again about the food. How lovely it all is. How plentiful it is. I do hope that she doesn't suffer too much, if and when this wretched war with the Nazi Government arrives. She is so young to have to live through these terrible times.

Pray for me. Our little son is lost. Let it please God, not to take Patrick from me as well.

Your loving sister,
Ellie.

Nancy's Story
Manchester
May 1938

'So, here he is working on this week's letter to the *Manchester Guardian*.'

'Will you leave your brother alone?'

Nancy dropped a brown paper parcel on the table. Dan pushed it away from his work.

'Two summer dresses and enough for a blouse for me.' She leaned over Dan's shoulder and read what he had written. 'What this?' she asked.

'We're moving house,' her mother said.

'What's Dan doing then? Informing the newspapers?'

'I'm drawing up a contract. For our new house. It's a bungalow, if you want to know. In Factory Lane.'

'Wouldn't you know. Wouldn't you just believe it? Move to a bungalow and everyone else moves to 'The Grove,' or 'Acacia Avenue,' but no, not us. We have to move to 'Factory Lane'. Perfect. And what's the new abode in Factory Lane like? Does it have a fifty-foot chimney stack? Is there a hooter instead a bell at the front door?'

'It's a lovely place,' Ellen said. 'And we'll be needing the garden, now the Dazzler is here.' She rocked the sleeping child. 'He needs a garden to play in and fresh air to breathe.'

'We managed without,' said Nancy.

Her mother ignored the remark.

'Besides, when's the child going back to his mother and father? What are we going to do then with our new palace? It's all very well for them to have another baby but if they expect us ...' She glanced at her mother. '... expect you to look after this one.'

'He's not going back,' Ellen said. 'Not for the present. Now will you stop your noise or you will be waking the little dote and Dan's trying to write his contract.'

'It's time for Patrick and Nancy Manuel to look after their own kids, not give them to you to care for. That's all I meant. Now, I've bought some potato cakes. Does everyone want one?'

The child in Ellen's arms stirred and rubbed his eyes with his fists. 'The little dote,' she said. 'The Dazzler.'

She gave the child a kiss on his forehead. 'Don't you be worrying. You're staying here. Your mammy has enough to do with baby number three taking all her time and before we know, baby number four will be along. You're staying here.' She patted the little child. 'Come on, Mickey Dazzler. There's a good boy and we'll let your Uncle Dan finish his contract though I don't know what good that is going to bring. If someone wants to evict us they'll find a way to do it.'

'The child wasn't disturbing me,' Dan said. 'And besides, I've finished. No one will get us out of the new place in a hurry and you'll have a fine home to live in, when I go off back to Ireland.'

'It does occur to me,' said Ellen. 'That when we move to our new home we'll be in need of some lovely new furniture.'

'Instalments.'

'What was that?'

'Easy terms. We can buy the furniture on easy terms.'

'I was thinking that we ought to buy it outright. Something a little special. You can't buy the quality stuff on the never-never.'

'We'll manage,' Dan said.

'The Dazzler will be needing a bed of his own. He's growing too big to sleep with Nell and me. He's always thrashing around. Trying to scratch that terrible eczema. He gets so restless. We don't want you to scratch that terrible eczema, do we?'

Ellen looked up from the sleeping child.

'It might seem cruel to keep his hands tight by his sides. It's a cruel way to stop him scratching, isn't it?' Ellen gave the child another kiss. 'But if we don't, he'll get another of those bad skin infections and we don't want that, do we?' She broke off for a moment. 'Never still a moment even when he is asleep. Are you, my darling boy?'

'Easy terms,' Dan said.

'I was thinking that it might be an ideal time to write to your father again.'

'We haven't seen him for years. We don't know where he is.'

'Barcelona. Larry let that slip, last time he visited. Your father is in Barcelona. Managing one of the best football teams in the world. That's what Larry said.'

'Barcelona is in the middle of a Civil War, Mother. I doubt Father would get any letters we might send him, let alone have money to spare for furniture, for the new house he's never likely to see.'

'It's a simple thought and you never know when he might come to visit and we need the house to look respectable.'

'We haven't seen him for twenty years.'

'Eighteen. It's eighteen years since you and I travelled to Newcastle upon Tyne to see him. You'll remember?'

'Not really but do go on.'

'With the Spanish Civil War raging all around him he may decide to come back, to have a proper home once more and live with us again.'

Dan concentrated on the papers set out on the table.

'Possibly, but you can get Nell to write that letter for you. Not me.'

'It was a thought,' his mother said. 'Now, I've got to get this child to bed.' She got to her feet, taking care not to disturb the little boy. 'Child of my heart. It's time for bed. We'll see if your Aunt Nell will write to your grandfather and ask for some money for a nice new bed for you and perhaps some lovely new furniture for us as well. What do you think?'

Tom Recalls His Early Visits
to the O'Connell Family Home
June 1938

At the Irish Club there was always good company and plenty of sport, though I never took to the boxing myself. Table tennis, that was my game. Once had a match with the Hungarian Olympic Lady Champion, Miss Guells, when she came to Manchester on an exhibition visit. A woman with such flair, such style. How she could play. To watch her win game after game was a sight to remember.

'Tom,' this fellow said. 'When am I going to get you to sign up for the football team?' No introduction. No name. Nothing. After a moment, by way of an explanation, 'At the night school.' He pointed to himself, 'Patrick,' he said. 'At the night school. We were in the same class.'

Always late to the class and not a word of apology to anyone. Patrick looking like he had slept in his clothes. The same every week until he left and that was before we had the examinations. 'No time for them,' he said. 'I've learned what I want. Don't need for anyone to tell me how much I know.' Though you'd not believe it, he was quite a clever fellow.

'The table tennis league, I play in that,' I said. 'Impossible to do both. It can't be done. The table tennis matches or the football training, they're on a Thursday evening. Can't play football without going to the training and that's on a Thursday evening as well.'

Patrick scribbled a note on the fixture list. 'And sure you can play in the table tennis team and the football league. I'll put you down for Inside Right.' That was his way. Didn't listen. Always did what he had set out to do, without great consideration for what suited others.

Patrick said his father had been a footballer. That's why the family had moved from Ireland, so his father could play for the English teams. Sheffield Wednesday, Hull City, Manchester United. 'Football. It's in my blood. There's no denying it. We'll give them a match they won't forget in a hurry. With the two of us playing, we can't lose. Tom, you're down for Inside Right. This next Saturday, 3:00 p.m. sharp. And don't be late in getting there.' That was great coming from him.

And the next moment Patrick was inviting me to his home. 'You must meet my family. My mother. My sisters. And Dan, my little brother.' No mention of the football-playing father. It was only later I found he had left the family and gone off abroad to Spain or some such place. And there was a hole where the footballer ought to have been, a great gaping hole and nothing seemed to fill it, though I didn't learn that for quite a while.

My first visit to Patrick's home in Church Street, it was his sister Nell who opened the door. Without doubt you will have heard of love at first sight. Some people may think it's not true, but I can swear on all that's Holy, it is. I'd have died for her. I'd have swum the Irish Sea for her. Beautiful, clever, self-assured, witty – there was no one like her anywhere. Before I left the house after that first meeting, I'd made up my mind to marry her, if she'd ever have me.

After that introduction you couldn't keep me away from the house. Called in after work just about every evening. When after some considerable time and a hundred visits, it occurred to me the name of the town of Salford was dropped into the conversation rather more times than you would expect in the normal run of things. Salford, it's a fine town and I wouldn't hear a word against it. Not so far away from where the family lived. Was it the location of a new discussion group? A consciousness-raising circle or whatever Nell and her brother Patrick had gone to? Their political lives were their own, the single area she and I didn't share with the same passion.

When yet another publication appeared on the kitchen table, I'd given it little thought. 'New writer working on the newspaper,' Nell said. 'There are one or two good articles he's had published. You'll find it's worth the time to read them.' To my thinking, it was such a turgid style used in those newspapers; the same sentiments expressed in twenty different ways. The imminent uprising of the workers. The victory of the proletariat. The forthcoming war against fascism. I skimmed through the pages and stopped here and there to show my interest. These views were of great importance to Nell. She held them with complete conviction. Then the usual end to the evening, time for a chaste kiss on the doorstep and a promise from me to call to see her the following day.

How could I be so slow? I stopped in the middle of the street. The man close behind walked into me. 'Want to look where you are going,' he muttered. 'Young …' What was in the newspaper articles Nell had encouraged me to read? The woman worker of the future was to be freed from the shackles of bearing infants without number. The families of the next generation were not to stagger under the burden of babies they were not able to feed. They would not be forced to toil to put a crust of bread in the mouths of yet more children. And where was this information available, if only for the married woman? It was clear. I understood. Outside of London I had read, Salford was the first place where that information was available, information helping women to protect themselves from never-ending childbirth. I now understood why Salford was of such importance.

Nell always knew what she wanted. It went without saying that married is only one step from almost married. She offered me intimacy without the dangers of lasting consequences, not that I'd have minded. I'd have got her to the altar without so much delay.

And so it was, Nell seduced me in the front parlour. Her mother was at the neighbour's and never back home before ten o'clock, Patrick at one of his political meetings, Dan who knows where, the Dazzler tucked up in bed. You might say I'd been slow to realise what was going on, though you must bear in mind I'd been raised in a good Irish Catholic household. The modern woman might enjoy this intimacy with little risk of a hurried marriage and a bundle of joy nine months later. Nell was mine for the taking and I, of course, was hers.

The British Consul's Letter from Barcelona to the O'Connell family in Manchester 11 July 1938

British Consulate General
Caldetas, Barcelona
11th July 1938

Mrs E. O'Connell
The Bungalow
75 Factory Lane
Blackley
Manchester

Madam

With reference to your letter of the 28th June enquiring about your husband, Mr Patrick O'Connell, I write to inform you that he called at this Consulate General on the 25th June. He seemed at the time to be in excellent health.

His address when he was last registered was given as: Calle Villamun No. 26, Les Cortes, Barcelona.

I am,
Madam,
Your obedient servant
J. M. Walsh
Acting Consul General.

Patrick's Letter from Barcelona
to His Brother Larry in London
October 1938

Larry

There's no water supply, no gas supply and the baker hasn't baked any bread for an age. Life here gets more difficult by the hour. Every time you step outside the house another rumour catches up with you. It does not cease to amaze me that things have continued for so long without completely falling apart.

I am writing this in the greatest of haste, as a neighbour is about to leave for France. His plan is to get across the frontier as quickly as possible. It is my intension to leave by the end of the week.

I will send this note with him in case I am unsuccessful in my attempt to get away. I managed to secure a place for Ellie on one of the British ships that have been taking off people from this hell on earth. It was the intention that she go to France and then to England. All being well …

They are leaving now.

I must finish.

When Ellie gets to London, look after her. I will do my best to join her there.

You have never failed me.

Your brother,

Patrick.

For the *International Monitor*
on the Road to the Spanish Frontier with France
November 1938

Our Correspondent

And still they come, in their hundreds, in their thousands. A grey trail of desperate humanity. An acrid dust rises, hanging over the crowd and is carried along with them as they walk. Each elderly man, (for there are few young men here, other than the wounded), each woman, forcing themselves to take the next step and the next step and the step after that, towards the land that offers them some hope of refuge. Each person struggles to get to the frontier before the Nationalist Armies catch up with them and as they walk, they know those armies are following hard on their heels.

A rumour spreads from mouth to mouth: The border is to be closed. People gather their last drop of energy and surge forward. They clutch their documents for the officials to check, brandish them in the air, even though those officials are a kilometre away. Those documents are passports or a visa issued by the Republican Government; a possible source of entry to France or a death warrant, if discovered by the Nationalists.

The rumour fades. The trail of humanity takes up a steadier pace. There are mothers carrying children in their arms, old people shuffling along, supporting each other. The fortunate few travel on the backs of lorries and carts. Most do not enjoy that luxury.

We struggle forward. I feel their dread, their exhaustion. Finally, we reach the frontier. I join the queue of humanity waiting to cross through the barrier. A border guard recognises me and waves me on. I have passed this way several times in the last few days. Guilt overwhelms me as I consider whether I will take advantage of this. I remonstrate with myself. It will mean one less person to process yet why ought I be treated differently to the others waiting there to have their papers checked.

People cluster around me to tell heart-breaking stories, of dead children, of missing soldier sons, of loss of homes and possessions, of hunger and fear. They tell of their rage that the Government, the elected government, was undermined and in the main, the rest of Europe and the United States has stood by and watched. 'Go,' they say. 'You go and tell our stories to the world. Don't let us be forgotten.'

An elderly couple have travelled to the frontier by hay cart. Their crime? To be union organisers in the textile factory where they both worked. If they remain behind they will at best be imprisoned, at worst shot as 'Reds'. They have to live, the old woman tells me. Their only son was killed at the Battle of the Ebro, but they have a daughter-in-law and a young grandson. The couple have never seen this child. After the death of their son, he is the reason they must survive.

The elderly couple believe the daughter-in-law and new grandson are in – and here the old man takes a crumpled piece of paper out of his jacket pocket and shows me an address. This address is in the French city of Lille. 'There are many textile workers, people like us.' The old man continues 'They have offered a sanctuary to fellow workers. They have given comfort and security to our daughter-in-law and our grandson. We will get there somehow. We will get to Lille, even if we have to walk.' His wife agrees as she wipes away a tear.

Close by there is a young woman. She stumbles forward. In her arms is a small child. A little boy clutches at her skirts. Her husband is missing, presumed dead. She wants to get to France where a cousin of hers is married to a French national of Catalan extraction and has offered her shelter. 'I'm going to fight the fascists when I'm older,' the little boy says. 'I'll be nine years old soon.'

Behind this family is a girl. She is leaning on a crutch. She is sixteen years of age, she tells me. Her ankle was broken and then badly set. 'At least I can walk,' she says. 'And I will get myself out of this country before the Nationalists arrive. I do not wish to live under their rule. They killed my parents and for what? They were both teachers. They were good people. Intellectuals.'

Small groups of refugees have their papers processed and one by one they step onto French soil. They at least feel they have escaped from the worst that a Civil War might do to them. Each of those people turn as they cross the border to take a last look at their beloved homeland; 'We will return.' They swear to themselves. 'We will return.'

Once over the frontier they move forward again and then many slump down to sit on the pavement at the side of the road. They at least have completed the first stage of their journey. The children shiver and lean against their mothers. The women know they must continue to be strong for what is ahead. Their priorities are to find something to eat and then somewhere to sleep, to gather strength for the morrow. First to the staging camps and then to whatever future they might find, in France, in Belgium, in Great Britain or further away, in South America.

What unites these people is the absolute certainty that they will return to their homeland, that the Nationalist Armies will be defeated and driven out and that they will be able to go back to the country they love.

1939

Dan's Story
Manchester
April 1939

The way into the hall was blocked by a pile of suitcases. His mother gave the door another push.

'When you get to Dublin,' Ellen called to Dan, 'you'll go finding you've got Willy and Aida's things with you. Not your own.'

Dan picked up a handful of luggage labels. 'There's no danger,' he said. 'None at all. I've got half a dozen of these.' He waved the labels above his head for his mother to see.

Willy stepped over a case. 'I'll be moving our luggage out of your way this moment,' he said. 'Aida wants to change her dress.'

'I only want to make myself presentable,' Aida said from the living room. 'Trust Willy to make an issue of it.'

'That is ours and so is that,' said Willy and pulled a suitcase through to the main room. Aida stood in the doorway watching her husband. 'Take care of your back,' she said. 'You go lifting that and you'll never get to Hull again.'

She turned to Ellen. 'I've told him a hundred times. I don't know what he puts in these cases.' She tapped the luggage with the tip of her toe.

'A dental drill,' Willy said. 'Second-hand. He was retiring. Didn't need it any more. A real bargain.'

'Think how long the previous one lasted. What a bargain that proved to be. We've had experience of your bargains before. Aida turned to Ellen again. 'Wouldn't you know. Can't find space for my clothes but plenty of room for a dental drill. And the last one your brother bought was useless. How long did that last?' she called across to Willy.

'And how do you expect me to continue to earn my living?' Willy replied. 'We've got to move forwards with the times. This was only bought last year. Brand new. On the boat –'

'Don't speak to me about the boat,' Aida said. 'All the conversation was about … Go on. You tell them, Willy.'

'War,' he said. 'Will we ever get to Ireland? Will we ever get back to England after the visit home? Can the aeroplanes the Nazis have fly as far as Dublin? That's all everyone could talk about. There's a war coming,' he said. 'And Ireland will be …'

'The submarines. You remember the submarines, don't you, Ellen?' interrupted Aida.

Ellen nodded. 'It was a terrible time,' she said. 'Terrible. The summer Nell was born. The Great War, it broke out two or three days later. And the others were little dotes, Young Patrick and Nancy and Dan of course, he hadn't been born yet and it was a horrible time to have to travel. I thought we were all going to end up at the bottom of the Irish Sea, I did.'

'There,' Aida continued. 'I told you Nell was born in Ireland. And what about you?' she said turning to Dan.

'Manchester,' he said. 'Though I've every right to live in Ireland with both my parents Dublin-born.'

'You go to Ireland,' Willy said. 'Within a year, months even, there's going to be another war. As bad as the last one, the Great War or whatever they care to call it. Worse, even. You mark my words.'

'God save us,' Ellen said.

'Go now or you'll never get back. We've seen all this before.' said Willy.

Ellen looked around, 'Where's the Dazzler?' she said.

'Still playing in the garden. Good as gold,' said Aida.

A ball bouncing against the kitchen door. 'Goal!' the child shouted.

'Four years old and already playing like his granddah,' said Aida. 'Have you heard from him lately?'

Willy moved another of the cases. 'Mind yourself, Aida. Let me get this through to the other room.'

His wife stepped back and held the door open. 'I was only asking,' she said to Willy. 'You know how she likes talking about him.'

'Careful, now,' said Willy and gave Aida a meaningful look.

'Dan. How do you intend to make your living when you get to Dublin?'

'Writing,' his nephew said. 'The best place in the world to write.'

'Much money in that?'

'Can't go against his nature,' said Ellen. 'All he's ever wanted to do. Since he was a child. And he's had a letter printed in the *Manchester Guardian*.

'Not much money in writing letters to newspapers,' said Willy.

'It's a start,' said Ellen. 'We all have to start somewhere. And Dan's been in a production at the Library Theatre. The Library Theatre in Manchester,' she added.

Aida was suitably impressed. 'Takes after his father, then?'

Willy turned to his wife, a puzzled look on his face.

'I mean to say,' said Aida.

'His father was a footballer and now he's a manager,' said Ellen.

'No,' said Aida, once more composed. 'No. Successful. That's what I was meaning.'

'He was a great footballer in his time and now he's a manager, of a very important football team.'

'Has anyone seen my jacket?' asked Willy. 'I'm sure I left it on the chair. Can't find it anywhere.'

'He's the manager of a very important major team,' Ellen continued. 'FC Barcelona.'

'I thought there was a war going on? In Spain,' said Aida.

'Wars everywhere,' said Willy. 'Dan's got the right idea. Going back to Ireland. To the peace of Ireland and the Irish ways.'

Dan agreed. 'That's what I intend to do,' he said.

'Nell wrote,' Ellen said.

'To her father?'

'No, Aida,' said Ellen. 'To the British Consul. In Barcelona. And he's safe and well. Though perhaps with the war, he'll be coming home.'

'The Consul wrote that?'

'Aida,' said Willy.

'I was only asking,' said Aida.

'He's safe and well and I believe he might come back to Manchester. To get away from the terrible troubles those poor people are having in Spain,' said Ellen. 'Away from all those dreadful goings on.'

'Then he can be bombed by the Nazis rather than by the Fascists,' said Dan.

'Makes a change,' said Willy.

Ellen went through to the kitchen. Aida followed her. 'It's time I got the Dazzler in from the garden,' she called. 'Then we can eat.'

Aida picked up some cutlery. 'I've heard there are plans to evacuate the children. To the countryside. If war comes,' she said.

'Mother won't let him go,' said Dan, tying the last of the labels on to his luggage. 'She dotes on that child. No grandson of hers is going to the countryside, even if there is a war on.'

'I can hear you talking there,' called Ellen. 'If a bomb drops on this house, we all go together. Never mind this evacuating children to I-don't-know-where. Now, someone please, put these place mats on the table and then we can serve the food.'

'I'll do that,' said Willy. 'I'm a modern man and not afraid of a bit of housework.'

'First I've heard of it,' said Aida.

'Dan,' said Willy, 'You can help. It'll be good practice for you. Back in Dublin you're going to have to do this for yourself, until you find a nice colleen to serve your food and warm your bed.'

'Watch your language, Willy,' said Aida. 'Don't forget there's a child in this house. Ellen's fetching him in now.'

Ellie's Letter from London
to Her Sister Mary in Ireland
May 1939

Mary, Mary

Patrick is here. I can't quite believe it, but he is.

Everything I had hoped for – other than our little son, of course – has come true. My prayers have been answered and my heart is content. Patrick is safe and we are together again.

Let me tell you how it happened. As soon as the Boat Train arrived in Victoria Station in London, we were met by supporters of the Spanish Republican Government. Assistance was offered to us poor exiles from the moment we got down from the train.

The representatives from the Emergency Committee were kindness itself and when my travelling companions told of my terrible loss, a nurse was on hand immediately. She is so committed to the Spanish cause as her fiancé has fought with the International Brigades. They are very genuine young people. Almost before I knew what was happening, I was taken away by bus to a nearby boarding house and offered medical attention.

These people have considered our every need and I cannot tell of the pleasure of sleeping in a bed with clean sheets, nor is it easy to tell of the delights of drinking a proper cup of tea and enjoying eating a hot meal after this most horrible journey.

All of us who arrive from Spain are registered, our names taken and the date of arrival recorded. This is to ensure that people are put back in contact with family and friends, who have been parted as they were escaping.

As soon as I regained a little strength after this most demanding of journeys, I travelled down to Wimbledon to join the family. It may seem foolish to you now, but I did not dare go to Argyle Street, to Larry's hotel in case there was bad news. After the speed and disorganisation of my departure, I feared the worst.

The family has been wonderful, welcoming me with open arms. Yet I found I could not rest for one moment, constantly thinking of Patrick and wondering whether he was safe, doing everything possible to find out the true situation. It was so difficult to remain calm.

The family tried to persuade me to wait before going up to London again until I had gained more strength but soon realised I could not put off my visit of enquiry any longer. So, I returned to the Committee Rooms within a few days of my arrival in London. For some reason, I had come to believe it would be easier to think of learning the worst amongst a group of strangers. These people were all able to understand what I was going through, as they were suffering something similar themselves.

In no time at all I had learned the life of the exile from Spain. We spend our time searching through the lists of recent arrivals and we speak to all those who might have the least scrap of information about our loved ones. What is happening? Is it possible that Spain will be lost to the Nationalists? Have you heard any information about … ? And so we go on. Everyone is hoping for good news, yet we are always fearing the worst.

At the start of the week, I decided that I could not rest but must return yet again to Victoria. It was impossible to keep away. I busied myself walking from the underground station to the offices, trying to plan what I would do during the day and how to keep myself from feeling depression and misery and despair.

Let me say that the offices of the committee rooms are in the most magnificent buildings, similar in many ways to those in Dublin, in Merrion Square. At the front of each house is an imposing flight of steps leading up to the main door. As I walked up these steps I heard a single word: 'Ellie'. I stood stock still. It was as if I were paralysed. For the briefest of moments, I thought I was imagining this. Could it be that it was a trick of my mind and the voice was in my head, as I so wanted to hear it? Yet it was Patrick. It truly was. You can imagine my joy and delight.

Patrick, like me, had come to search the lists of new arrivals and seek any small piece of news. We hugged each other and then before we knew what was happening, we were surrounded by fellow exiles, shaking our hands and patting us on the back. Our reunion had brought some happiness to their lives. We were together again after our flight from Spain. For a brief moment we were all able to forget our pain and the disaster which daily unfolds there.

I have to confess that the warmth we felt that day from the people in the Committee Rooms has served to convince me the ordinary people in Britain are not as dry and cold as they are generally made out to be.

So, we are together again. For the moment Patrick continues at Larry's and will remain there for the next few days. It is then our intention to come over to join you all in Ireland while we consider what we will do next.

Yours in this moment of great joy and not a little sorrow.

Your sister

Ellie.

Patrick of course, knew nothing of our great loss. At the top of the steps he simply looked me up and down for a moment and shook his head. With that he accepted that our little son was no more. There was no need to give a detailed explanation. Then we were surrounded by other exiles and the moment passed.

Nell's Diary
Manchester
July 1939

Yesterday Dan's first letter from Ireland arrived. After telling us a thousand times he was going to settle there, it still seems difficult to believe he has finally gone and done so.

As yet he hasn't found a garret to live in, though he is looking into the possibility of taking lodgings overlooking the River Liffey. For the moment he's sleeping on the sofa in a friend's flat. At least we have an address to reply to.

When Dan's letter arrived I knew Mother was delighted. She was bright and cheerful all day. Even though she likes us to believe she doesn't care at all, I could see it in her face that she does. 'And you'll be sending your brother a ten shilling note when you reply,' she said, as always caring about the welfare of others.

What with the ten shillings for Dan and the money to pay for the specialist for the Dazzler, I've taken a second job in addition to my office work. Now on Saturdays from 9.00 a.m. to 1.00 p.m., I wrap parcels. People receive brochures by post and from these they select clothing, which they then order from their homes rather than travel to the shops. It's our job to wrap the clothes in brown paper packages and tie them up, ready for posting. The string is rough and, after tying dozens of knots, my fingers do throb.

It's dull, repetitive work though my fellow workers are cheerful enough. In the main their conversation does however, focus on 'my young man'. Even the coming war is seen in terms of whether he'll propose before he's called up and whether it will be possible to buy material for a wedding dress. Half the girls have never even heard of Dostoyevsky, let alone read him.

The only books that seem to appeal to my fellow workers are romances; the rich boy falls in love with the poor girl and rescues her from a life of poverty and drudgery. This is exactly what Nancy has always wanted, always dreamed of and look where it's got her.

To relieve Saturday mornings, I intend to observe the girls and use this experience in a short story I plan to write. On Dan's recommendation, I intend to watch what is happening around me more closely. He has already started work on his first novel and has some ideas for a play.

Apparently, the talk in Dublin is as in Manchester of the inevitability of war between Britain and Nazi Germany, whatever Mr Chamberlain has to say. Who in Dublin and all Ireland for that matter doesn't have family or friends in Britain? It seems certain no one will escape this conflict, even if Ireland is officially a neutral country.

The prevailing political situation does make me wonder what will happen to us all. I've made up my mind to go to the next performance of opera here in Manchester, whatever it might be, in case the performances are cancelled for the duration.

I also have to ask myself whether Dan's letters will get through to us here in England. Will the postal service between Britain and Ireland continue when the war begins? This makes me determined to send ten shillings as soon as possible, in case it is the last money I am able to send for months or even for years.

It seems the Dazzler is missing his Uncle Dan and often asks where he is. For his part, his Uncle Dan has more interest in the child's welfare than his own father and mother. We haven't heard from Pat and Nancy Manuel in weeks, yet they only live ten minutes walk away.

I must end here as it is getting late and it is possible paper will soon be in short supply. If this is the case what will happen about books? Will printing and publishing cease? What will happen about brown paper parcels for that matter?

We will have to find out. What I am certain about is that the poor will suffer more than the rich. That is always the case. The way of the world, as is said by some.

Patrick and Ellie's Story
Ireland
August 1939

There was noise coming from the bedroom and Patrick could be heard walking around up there.

'Will you come on downstairs. We're all waiting for you.' called Ellie. 'It's only a photograph and everyone else is ready.'

'You know I can't be doing with this,' Patrick called back.

'You must have had a thousand photographs taken. All those matches. All those teams. Now will you come down and join us?' Ellie continued the conversation from the hall.

Someone shouted from the garden.

'We're ready. We're ready.' Ellie called back and turned to wait for Patrick. 'You know how he fancies himself as a professional, since he bought that new camera. Have you any idea how much it cost? With all those special lenses and that carrying case. Come on now. Do your best.'

Outside in the garden the family group was organised, reorganised and then commanded to smile.

'Hurry up, will you? You'd have paint drying faster,' one of the group said.

The children began pushing each other.

'Keep yourselves still, will you?' said one of the women. 'Otherwise you can go in the house.'

One of the boys struck a pose like a circus strong man, his fists clenched and his arms flexed up to his shoulders.

'You'll stay like that if the wind changes,' said the woman, then turned to Patrick. 'I expect you are used to this. The photographs, I mean. In the newspapers, all the time.'

'We want Patrick to be interviewed for the *Journal*,' said her husband. 'It's of more than local interest. Having the manager of a top foreign football team back in the country.' The conversation was interrupted as the group was ordered to reform a little to the left of their original position.

'Quiet, please everyone. Hold it. Hold it,' ordered the photographer. 'There, you can all relax now.' The children started to run around again.

'I wasn't smiling,' said one little girl. 'He was pushing me and I didn't have time to smile.'

Her mother shook her head in exasperation. 'How long does it take you to smile?' she asked, 'Give me a moment and let me talk to Ellie. We haven't seen her for a long time and I want to talk to her.'

She turned to Ellie. 'What were we saying before?' she asked.

'He's a very private person, when he's away on holiday.' said Ellie. 'Aren't you, Patrick?' She included her husband in the conversation. 'I thought you wouldn't mind telling the men some of your football stories while we are setting the table for lunch. They're always asking what you are doing, who are the best players, when the Spanish team is going to come over here to Ireland to play.'

The photographer tried to reassemble the group. 'That last photograph. I'm not sure about the light.' He readjusted the lens.

'Children, still please. Patrick, move a little. To the left. No, to your left. We can scarcely see you there. Brigid, step forward a little. Good. Hold it. On the count of three. Lovely.'

The camera clicked and a general groan went up from the group.

'Enough. Enough. Lunch, please.'

Children ran around, chasing each other. The women moved towards the kitchen.

'No, Brigid, not you. Go and sit down. We can manage without you. You need to take it easy at the moment. Remember what the doctor said. Go and sit down. We eat in fifteen minutes, everyone.'

As Ellie walked towards the kitchen door, Patrick caught her eye.

'I'm alright,' she said, 'Really I am.'

'It's not easy for you. With Brigid.'

'I'm alright, truly.'

One of the men came across the lawn to Patrick.

'Are you going back?' he asked. 'To Spain. Now the fascists have won?'

'A better place, with the communists defeated,' said the man's brother-in-law.

'Better for whom?' the first man asked and the conversation turned to politics.

1940

Patrick's Letter from Seville
to His Brother Larry in London
March 1940

Larry

Finally, we have arrived here in Seville after a journey of nightmare proportions. All told it took at least four times as long to complete, as it would have done in the past. Don't doubt me or think that I exaggerate. It was hell in the doing but now we have arrived.

We crossed the frontier from France at Hendaye (more of this later) then travelled across to Barcelona, a painful and slow journey. It was appropriate to make this our first stop to enable us to rescue anything that remains from our former home.

It was with a thousand delays, we finally reached that once-proud city, now but a shadow of its former self. I recognise we disagree over matters of politics, yet I have to say to you the joy and beauty that was this magnificent place has been wiped away by this cruel war.

Certainly, the people might now go to Mass again, you will be delighted to learn, but they do so with fear in their eyes and hunger on their faces. It must be asked how long it will take for this phoenix to rise again from the ashes. One generation? Two generations? Not in my lifetime, I fear.

As we progressed across the country we suffered a painful series of train journeys, waiting on platforms for trains that never arrived, then we sat on trains that never moved for hours and hours. Ellie was quite despondent – so unlike her.

It was a terrible moment to arrive at our old home once more. You will remember the address in Les Corts, where we used to live when we first moved here, so close to the football ground of FC Barcelona.

The city has been ravaged. A vicious war has swept back and forth across it. Brother has fought brother. The Nationalists have triumphed for now, rampaging through the region to the very frontier with France and the frying pan I left on the stove when I fled was still there where I left it. The food was a little greener and the pan a little blacker but there it remained to be seen as such. An incredible thing, do you not think?

After Barcelona we moved on slowly to Madrid, where we took a short break to gather our strength for the final stage of our journey. We had been told there was more chance of us getting on a train if we travelled via the Capital. Here, as in Barcelona there are terrible signs of war; buildings gutted by fire, buildings pockmarked by bullet holes, devastation and deprivation everywhere. Look around and there are infinite signs that this beautiful country has torn itself apart.

I must take you back to Hendaye and our frontier crossing. The town is a sad sight with people still leaving Spain and arriving in a country which expects daily to be invaded by the Nazis. People huddle in groups on street corners, waiting for something to happen. People wait and wait and expect something, anything. They are bored but grateful that nothing is happening. War is a terrible thing.

There completely by chance, Ellie met with someone she knew from her days as a nanny. There is a small group of foreign diplomats living in the town with some of their wives and staff. They have been moved here to avoid the strife of the Civil War and to meet the needs of their countrymen, who continue to flee the Generalísimo's Spain. The meeting prompted great exclamations and amazement, as it was several years since Ellie had last seen this lady. The woman marvelled at why we wanted to re-enter Spain when, as you might imagine, the traffic is almost entirely in the opposite direction.

It is a sad world. Herr H is now officially held in high regard. His virtues are expounded daily on the radio and in the press. The Spanish people are being urged to yet more deprivations to support their Heroic Allies in the Fight Against the Red Hoards. Such is life.

Now Larry, it is your turn to live in a country at war, albeit this time with a foreign enemy. You might not be so keen on those who fight the Godless Reds when Herr H rains his bombs down on London.

Do not be surprised if some of our letters arrive from France or from Portugal or were even posted in London. This will be due to the assistance of friends.

Whatever, I remain in affection

Your brother,

Patrick.

Once again we have been fortunate to find a house close to the football grounds. Our home is opposite Real Betis de Sevilla. I am back with my old team. We live close to pleasant tree-lined streets. The world here is however, a darker place.

The season has started well despite a lack of footballs, of boots, of boot studs, of shirts, of shorts etc. etc. etc.

Patrick's Letter from Seville
to His Brother Larry in London
December 1940

Dear Larry

This letter is being written with the utmost speed – Ellie knows someone who will get this out of the country for us when the family leaves for the Christmas holidays.

Little news gets through to us here. What does get reported must be treated with care and it has to be said, our skills at reading between the lines develop week by week.

We are told London is a smouldering ruin and our Heroic Friends in the Fight against Communism are on the brink of invading Britain. The newsreels show the Führer in Paris admiring the Eiffel Tower, all that beautiful city at his feet. Am I to see something similar with Herr H standing outside the Houses of Parliament or in Trafalgar Square? If he gets that far, will he cease his expansion plans or is the next stop the shores of Galway?

In preparation for Herr H's forthcoming visit to meet the Generalísimo, Himmler was sent on ahead to scout out the land. We have been treated to a news film of Himmler being driven along the main thoroughfare of Madrid with full pomp and circumstance and the buildings decorated with swastika flags. Crowds apparently lined the route showing spontaneous enthusiasm for this visit. Needless to say, there was no mention of the day off work with full pay the (tame) unions had organised for the masses to enjoy.

Only a month later his boss Herr H himself, dained to come to our frontier with France – the most recent territory in his empire. It has to be asked whether the Spanish people are up to joining in with his mad plans. Doesn't Herr H realise these poor people are already worn out after years of deprivation and fratricidal struggle?

If indeed half London lies beneath the rubble and the population has fled in terror, there is little chance this letter will ever reach you. Should life be marginally better and this note does arrive – better to reply immediately, as the person who delivers the letter will bring the reply to me on his return to Spain.

In this time of great trouble, Ellie sends you her best regards.
Your brother,
Patrick.

This ill-humoured letter would get me shot if discovered. It is an angry note made worse by lack of food. What is happening in London? And in Dublin? Do you know?

1941

I am now an official fire watcher. Yesterday, I wore my boiler suit for the first time. It's navy blue in colour, large and uncomfortable. Mother managed to get it without using any clothing coupons. It's supposed to be second-hand. So, with my overalls and tin helmet, I'm ready to fight fascism wherever it might appear.

Fortunately, it was quiet last night. A blessing I have to say, as I've no desire to spot incendiary bombs nor put out small fires using a stirrup pump and a bucketful of water. My fellow fire-watcher Ted seems disappointed by the lack of activity. I suspect he hankers after a repeat of the Christmas blitz.

Ted hasn't been called up to join the army as his brothers have, as he suffers from mild epilepsy. One would think he would be glad to have a valid reason to escape the Armed Forces but no, he wants his share of the action. He seems to regard the war as a boys' own adventure.

I have to say he's a good sort really and has brought a primus stove with him to the office along with a supply of methylated spirits. It's proving to be an asset already as on three fire-watching evenings lately, there has been no gas supply, due to ruptured pipes and hence no cups of tea.

A neighbour has promised Mother she will be able to get an extra eight ounces of sugar for us by Saturday – her brother-in-law works at the docks. I have to say I wouldn't mind a spoon or two of sugar right now, as I can't abide sugarless tea. Thinking about it though, the sugar ought to be kept for Tom. He worked six twelve-hour shifts last week and expects to do the same again this week. The factory is speeding up production and now the time to build a warplane from start to finish has been reduced by fifteen minutes. It is such a demanding job and Tom needs all the energy he can get.

It's strange to be married. Even now I still find myself going into the back bedroom at night, though it's more than three months since Mother and I swapped rooms. 'You're a married woman. That room is yours by right.' So, there it was. I have moved into the front bedroom, where Tom and I now sleep.

Married. Me. I can't believe it. And married in a church, as well. A Registry Office would have been fine, but Tom's mother had very definite ideas on that. We were to have 'a proper wedding' and a church wedding was what we got. Nancy made me my dress with a matching muff and Tom's brother walked me down the aisle.

'You've known him for nine years. Don't you think it's about time you married him?' said Paddy. He had thought I was nervous but he was wrong. With each step I took as I walked up the aisle, I thought of Father. By rights, he ought to have been there, offering me his arm, taking me to the altar, giving me away. But no, it was not to be.

Since then a day doesn't go by without my thinking of Father. He keeps coming into my thoughts. Did he survive the Civil War in Spain? What would he think of my getting married? Would we recognise each other if we were to meet? I don't suppose we would.

And naturally, whenever I think of Father, I think of Spain and with all the rationing that's started I thought of oranges. I've read the streets of Spain are lined with orange trees and you can pick the fruit on the way to work. With that I started to hanker after an orange. I could taste the sweet, juicy segments. Foolishly, I mentioned this, that I would love to eat an orange. Immediately, Tom's mother thought I was expecting. I've told Tom there won't be any children, what with Mother and the Dazzler – 'his ready-made family,' Tom calls it – we can't manage any more. It's the expense. That's enough, with Mother and the Dazzler. Enough and no more, as they say.

After an age, Ted came back with two mugs of tea. He was full of the news that there's an unexploded bomb near his home. He'd just been told the story by one of the secretaries who stopped by – in a state of great excitement, I don't doubt – thrilled to be able to deliver the details. The war had come to his doorstep. He seemed delighted by this. I felt his excitement was out of place.

As spring is coming the days are getting longer and what with double summertime, I wanted to make the most of the daylight. I hoped to read to pass the time when I wasn't trying to spot any fires and burning buildings. Unfortunately, Ted wanted to talk. He went on for ages until he had to go down stairs to speak to one of the air-raid wardens. Then I was left to enjoy a bit of peace and quiet. The book was distracting, yet despite this, I found my mind wandering.

I thought of Father, Father bringing the car back from the factory where he worked during the Great War and spending the afternoon driving up and down the street, so that everyone might have a ride in the motor. Father waving to us as we left Scotland and came back to Manchester. The money he sent from Spain and how good it was when we didn't have to hide from the rent man and were able to pay the moneylender a little of what we owed. The money from Spain that meant Mother would buy cakes for tea and we could put some coal on the fire. It's not been easy. It will be better with Tom.

United Press International
News Report: Santander
Late 1941

Direct news from Franco's Spain remains under embargo, consequently this report comes to you from our correspondent, somewhere in Europe.
Reports are reaching us here of a major fire that has swept through the coastal city of Santander in North West Spain.

Eyewitness accounts tell of five- and six-storey buildings burning out of control. One resident who wouldn't give his name, told of desperate parents dropping their children from third and fourth floor windows. Neighbours stood below waiting to catch the infants in outstretched blankets. Chains of local people passed buckets full of water from hand to hand in a vain attempt to subdue the conflagration.

After months of limited rainfall the fire spread rapidly through the tinder dry buildings. A stiff breeze fanned the flames sufficient to allow them to leap across entire streets and rage without control.

Much of the old quarter of the city and the port area was destroyed by the fire. Entire blocks of flats, businesses and shops have been reduced to cinders. Even a week after the first fire broke out the rubble still continued to smoulder.

The total number of casualties remains unknown, though is thought to be high. Yet more victims are expected to succumb to their injuries in the coming days.

Officially, this disaster is said to be the work of the 'Reds'. Unofficially, I was told there exists a chronic shortage of fire fighting equipment and of trained fire fighters.

1943

Patrick's Letter from Seville
to His Brother Larry in London
April 1943

Dear Larry

An acquaintance of Ellie's is to leave the country soon, so we foreigners are taking advantage to send out some mail.

The city of Seville, indeed the entire area of Andalucia is awash with rumours and counter-rumours. Apparently, the body of a British diplomat has been caste up on the shores close to the city of Huelva, (some 60 miles from here). It would seem he was on a mission, his aeroplane was shot down and he was drowned.

What the grapevine also informs us of is that the man had plans of great importance – carried in a briefcase handcuffed to his wrist. The whisper has it these plans were a copy of the Allied Invasion of Europe. Whatever, within no time one or two of the local high-ups were away to Madrid and doubtless, to continue on to the Reich. It is to be imagined a copy of the plans went with them to Berlin.

It would appear the Generalísimo still maintains some fond hopes Herr H might yet win this war. Here was an additional opportunity to curry favour with the Axis powers.

To counter this, certain people regard this entire event as an indication the Allies will continue with the European invasion and not stop at the Spanish borders. If fascism is to be defeated through Europe, why halt at the Pyrenees? Does the body of this man indicate forces massing close to these frontiers to implement this?

Here we struggle by on a daily basis. I imagine your lot must be similar. Does anything of Argyle Street remain standing? Have Herr H's plans for invasion and total victory caused the entire city of London to be obliterated?

It never ceases to fascinate me that the Capital and environs were reduced to ruins in 1940, in 1941 and again recently. Am I to presume a major building programme was carried out in the intervening period? If it has been made rubble once, how might this happen again and again? The official press here forgets itself.

News has also reached us that the Nazis have bombed Dublin. Is this true? If you have any details, let us know what has happened. Ellie is most concerned.

As the foreign community is much reduced at present, it is highly probable I will have to attend the funeral of this unknown man. We foreigners are all grouped together, wherever we are from. Life throws up strange events at times. Who would ever have expected that I might have to go to the funeral of a British diplomat lost in the seas off the coast of Spain?

Ellie wants me to attend the funeral to pray for the soul of the departed – more your area than mine, I must say. However, there are few of his countrymen available to do this last act for him. And of course, one never knows what one might discover, even at a funeral.

This letter is brief – paper is in short supply.

I remain as ever,

Your brother,

Patrick.

It will also give me an opportunity to buy some strawberries. The Spring arrives early in the south of Spain and the best strawberries – the size of plums and deliciously sweet – come from Huelva.

1945

Ellie's Letter from Seville
to Her Sister Mary in Ireland
September 1945

Dear Mary

There is something I would like to ask you regarding a Hollywood film that is very popular here. The film is called 'Casa Blanca' and stars Ingrid Bergman and Humphrey Bogart. Do you know the film? Has it been released in Ireland yet? Or in England? If you have seen this film, please sort something for me.

Is it true in the original version of the film that Ingrid Bergman is married to Victor Lazlo, yet falls in love with Humphrey Bogart? I've watched the film four times – most recently on Saturday last – and am most perplexed. Here in Spain the sound track of the film indicates that Ingrid Bergman is the sister of Victor Lazlo not his wife. The story line is that Ingrid Bergman is so devoted to her brother that she cannot tear herself away from him to be with the man she loves.

Neighbours who have seen the film ask if this is indeed what happens in the original version. We do know the censor has had his hands on this. As I am one of the few to have contact with the world beyond Spain, people turn to me to confirm or deny what is happening. I trust this is not too much trouble for you.

Naturally, Patrick would not come along to see the film with me and, as for any changes in the story line, he asks me what do I expect with the power of the morality police (as he terms the film censors).

I've looked carefully at the faces of the film actors and feel Patrick may well be right and that the script has been rewritten for the benefit of the Spanish audience. Ingrid Bergman only speaks of her brother when she is facing away from the camera. It would offend the delicacies of Franco's supporters if Ingrid Bergman, as a married woman, were to be in love with someone other than her husband. Do let me know which version is correct. Is Victor Lazlo Ingrid Bergman's brother or her husband? I now fully suspect the latter.

Recently, Patrick has been saddened to learn of the confirmation of the death of Josep Sunyol. You might remember he was director of FC Barcelona when Patrick moved to the Club. His death was most mysterious. He was reported to have gone to live abroad and survived the Civil War, but Patrick has always believed that he was killed just as the Civil War broke out. Patrick felt his commitment to FC Barcelona and to Catalonia was so great it would be impossible for him to leave at such a time. It is likely his car strayed into Nationalist territory and he was killed for the fault of being in the wrong place at the wrong time. His status as a diplomat did not save him.

Patrick says they (meaning the present government) have even stolen his name; he is referred to as José Suñol, the Spanish version of his name, not the Catalan version by which we knew him. In the new order, Catalan is forbidden and people are not to speak using this language. Josep's poor family. How they have suffered over the years. Now perhaps his soul may rest in peace.

I'm quite running out of paper. So little is available at present and here I am asking about a film. Still, it is that several people are looking forward to your reply, not only me.

I look forward to your next letter.

Your loving sister,

Ellie.

Of course there were no celebrations here, for the successful conclusion of the war by the Allied powers. Patrick says it is likely the Generalísimo had worked for the Allied victory all along or that is what we will be told.

1950

Don Ricardo Cabot Montalt
Trainer's Certificate
Madrid
January 1950

CONFIRMS:

That Don Patrick O'Connell has attended the special course to qualify as a Football Manager, organised by the Royal Spanish Federation and celebrated in Madrid from 2nd to 5th of the present month, having been accredited with achieving the required standard.

It might be seen that from this day forward that he is entitled to use the appropriate title, signed the fifth of January, One Thousand, Nine Hundred and Fifty.

Ellie's Letter from Seville
to Her Sister Mary in Ireland
January 1950

Dear Mary

Happy New Year! Happy 1950!

It was a true pleasure to receive the Christmas card from you, along with the accompanying letter.

After the festivities of the season (subdued though they were), life is quiet here once again; with Patrick away to Madrid, the more so.

This country is sinking in a morass of paperwork. Everything we do (and by 'we' I mean everyone here in Spain), requires form filling and it must be stamped by at least three different officials and the offices are open at different times. Some of our friends say this form filling is done to create more jobs for the unemployed, others say it is done to weed out any remaining Reds. Documents are checked against lists of the surnames of wanted men.

In Patrick's case it is to comply with the new legislation and I don't know what. He has to qualify as a football trainer. Yes, you have understood me correctly. After almost 30 years in this country and having trained some of the best teams to victory, a training qualification is now demanded of him.

Truly, it has caused Patrick no little distress, though he has been stoical about it. In reply to my protestations, he says it is only a piece of paper that is needed of him and besides he will enjoy three or four days in Madrid, where he has to go for his training. Training the trainer – in other circumstances, it would make me laugh. He would be able to train those so-called trainers a thousand times over.

Fortunately, there is an event ahead to brighten Patrick's life. The World Football Cup is to be resumed and will be played in Brazil. Since Patrick made the Tour of Mexico all those years ago, he has continued to say the Latin American teams are emerging giants and they will be able to challenge the Europeans in no time. Listen to me! The footballer's wife!

The situation here remains difficult. Food is scarce and the markets are almost empty. Money goes nowhere and everything one buys to eat is so expensive. However, I must not complain. All I have to do is think of how pained I felt when it was likely that Patrick was gone forever. What does the price of coffee matter in circumstances like that? And there are many women here who are in a far worse situation than I am.

Seville is cold and damp – not at all what you would expect in the 'frying pan of Europe'. Thank God the winters here are short. In my next letter you can guarantee I'll be complaining about the heat and longing for some good old-fashioned rain to keep down the dust.

Enough.

Do write to me soon and send me all your news.

With much love,

Ellie.

Dan's Story
Dublin
June 1950

Another ball of paper ricocheted across the room. It rolled towards his companion and stopped at his feet.

'Leave it,' Dan said. 'Leave it where it is.'

Michael ignored him and picked it up. He flattened out the page and read the opening lines. '"Dear Father, I imagine this letter will come as a surprise to you." Shock might have been a better choice of word.'

'Pass it back.'

'And why is that then?'

'I want to finish it.'

'This will have to be the third one you've started.'

'Fourth,' Dan said.

'And how many more will you be planning to write before you finish a single one of them?'

'Consider it. It's a difficult thing to do, to write to someone you haven't seen for thirty years.'

'You haven't heard anything from him for half a lifetime?' Michael said.

'Do you mind? Letters used to arrive from Spain.'

'There was I thinking he never wrote to you.'

'Well, envelopes rather than letters, to be truthful. An envelope would arrive from Spain and there was money in it.'

'No letter?'

'That's what Mother used to tell us, only Spanish money. No letter. That's what she always told us; money but no letter and then Nell and I would go and change the Spanish pesetas into English money.'

'Your Mother let you change the money?'

'That was Mother for you. It was holiday time when the money arrived. Nell and I would buy sweets and cakes and cigarettes for Mother and then we wouldn't have to hide from the debt collectors for a week or two. Cigarettes and sweets and cakes and then it would be back to normal and she'd send Nell or me to the door to get rid of the rent man. Pay a little off and then make the rent man and the others wait for the rest. I hated it. They ... the rent man, the debt collector, the man who had the corner shop, they always knew when we had got an envelope from Spain. Everyone in the neighbourhood knew. Nobody else got letters, let alone letters from a foreign country. But we got our cakes and sweets and that was Mother for you.'

Dan stood up. 'Cup of tea?' he asked.

He turned the tap on full and then stepped back from the sink to avoid the spray. The water dripped onto the floor.

'Shite,' he said. 'Where's the cloth? It's a strange thing, but I always knew that Father would be well-known in Spain. The Spanish people, they would all know who he was.'

'Do they know?'

'They do. At the very least, the footballers do. Father in Spain and us growing up in Manchester and Mother begging and borrowing and the letters arriving with money and suddenly, it was holiday time and some of the dark depths of poverty would disappear.'

'Don't lose that.'

'What?'

'Dark depths of poverty.'

'It's something writers never get. Sure they talk about it but how many of them know what it is really like? The depths of misery – the cold and the damp and eating bread and dripping when you loath every mouthful but you are famished hungry and the shame of avoiding the people your family owe money to and Nell feeling proud because she knew how to pronounce "Santander". No, they don't get that.'

'He lives there?'

'Where? Santander?'

'He did, before he moved to Seville.'

'We had an old priest who had lived in Seville. He would talk about it as the most beautiful city in the world. The galleons would arrive there from the Americas loaded with treasure. At the time of the Conquest.'

'What's that?'

'Seville. The galleons, with those huge sails, arrived there from the Americas loaded with gold and silver.'

'Then Larry said he moved to Barcelona. Mother made Nell write to him. By then I was old enough to know better and she wanted us to ask for money. Can you believe it? Money. After all that time. I imagine he was delighted to get that letter.' Dan pushed his chair back from the table. 'I want to meet him and ask him why he left.'

'So when you've written this letter, you intend to post it? And you expect to get a reply?'

'I do intend to post it and I expect a reply.' The gas ring made a popping sound.

'It might give him a heart attack. A letter from the son he hasn't seen for decades. The past he had thought forgotten, coming creeping up on him again.'

'It might give his new wife a heart attack as well.'

'You expect him to have a new wife? I thought your Mother would have lasted him a life time.'

'Please,' said Dan. 'I've always been given to understand that he was a man for the ladies since the days of his youth. He won't be living the life of a monk now. It stands to reason.'

'How did you know that?

'How do you think? Larry. He knew and he was hinting so that Mother knew he knew, if you follow. She put up with his visits to Manchester and his hints because she felt sure that there would be some money in it for the family. A ten shilling note or something like that, when he left.'

The water boiled. Dan went over to pick up the kettle.

'They were always the same, the visits. Mother believing Larry had come to spy on the family, to give a report back to Father, but she would put up with it because there would be a ten shilling note for us before he went back to London. Larry never got on with Mother. He said she was reckless with money and he didn't approve.'

'Besides the new wife might be Spanish.'

'And?'

'And so not able to read the letter written in English.'

'A possibility, certainly.' Dan poured the boiling water into the teapot. 'My God but I hated bread and dripping,' he said, sitting down again and pulling another sheet of paper towards him.

'It was easy to go to the football match. A simple thing to speak to the players afterwards and it was straightforward to ask if anyone in Spain in the game of football went by the rather unusual name of O'Connell but put pen to paper and it's different altogether.'

'You're supposed to be the writer,' Michael said.

'And?'

'It ought to be easy to write a letter.'

'You'd think so.'

'And if he replies? Do you intend to go to Seville?'

'If he replies, we go to Seville.'

Michael picked up his jacket. 'Write to him. No interruptions. I'm going for a walk. Forget the pot of tea.'

'What's that?'

'It's all right. Forget it. Just forget it.'

1951

Ellie's Letter from Seville
to Her Sister Mary in Ireland
March 1951

Dear Mary

Thank you for your lovely long letter. It was a true delight to hear from you.

As you can see we are in Seville once more. The return to Santander was difficult and didn't go as Patrick had expected, so here we are again back in the South.

It seems as Patrick says, the world is moving on. His style and training does not suit the younger generation and it certainly doesn't suit the new directors of many of the clubs. If you ask me, they have got the jobs not because of what they know but who they know and, of course, they are supporters of Franco to a man. A nice little job for them, even if they know nothing about sport.

Patrick's life continues focused on the football. He goes to the matches and meets with the older men who used to play for the teams he managed. Now he has turned his skills to looking for the players of the future, those young men who will have the ability to do well when they are older. The job doesn't pay much but it helps us get by. Fortunately, this work keeps Patrick busy, as he has been a little down in spirit since our return here. He says his age is weighing on him.

There are however several bright spots on the horizon. Recently, Patrick got a letter from a nephew of his. Can you believe it, after all this time? Mind the next generation is making its way in the world. I'd almost forgotten Patrick had a family other than Larry and the sister who emigrated to New Zealand. That's what comes of being one of nine children – you never get to know all of the family, especially all the nephews and nieces. I believe the young man is planning to come to Spain on a touring holiday and would like to meet up with his uncle. I wonder if he will want to stay with us or will stay in a hotel.

I always get concerned when we have visitors, not that we have many of them. Food is so expensive here – you wouldn't believe the price of meat and coffee – and I am not sure what people make of the simple fare we eat.

Myself, I've just had a delightful afternoon at a neighbour's home, sitting on the veranda drinking iced tea. There is already a hint of the summer heat. We had gathered there to help the daughters of the family prepare their dresses for the ferias. No doubt I've told you about these before but as they never cease to amaze me, I'm sure you will humour me if I repeat myself. There is nothing like this anywhere in the world and my poor description does not do them justice.

The young people are particularly excited about everything and there is much speculation as to what will happen and who will be there and for the families not a little matchmaking takes place. Small tents and cabins for food and wine and for all the goings on of the fair, are set up in the main parks and everyone but everyone will join in the events. It is quite delightful, the more so as this all takes place close to where we live.

This is of such importance the neighbour's daughters chatter on about it for weeks beforehand. How lovely their dresses are. How they will wear their hair. Which mantilla will be the best for the day and which for evening wear. I get quiet caught up with their excitement.

For those of our years it is truly exhausting but also a great pleasure. People from all over the area pour into Seville, some in carriages, others in carts, many on foot. The women look spectacular in their dresses, figure-hugging to the hips, then flowing down to the ankle in cascades of material. This is of such bright colours: yellows and reds and blues – eye catching and very beautiful. The women wear their hair oiled and tied up in a bun at the nape of the neck. They have a high comb set on the crown of the head and a mantilla draped over this. Often the women will also have beautiful embroidered shawls over their shoulders, to complete the costume. It is enchanting. Quite spectacular.

The young men ride magnificent horses, the horses' coats polished like steel and the men themselves groomed to perfection. Everyone parades around in his or her finery and there is much singing, guitar music and dancing until dawn. Some of these dances are very passionate and they rather surprised me when I first saw them performed, but now I recognise them as the true spirit of Andalucia. The crowds only clear at first light and then simply to rest to gather strength for the events of next day, when there is more singing, dancing and music and it all takes place over again. Can you imagine me up 'til the dawn'?

So here we are preparing for the coming ferias, to fill us full of the joy that returns to this country.

I will write to you again to let you know how these days of delight unfold.

Your loving sister,

Ellie.

Dan's Story
Seville
May 1951

The tram swung round the corner and travelled along the boulevard. It continued on in its stop-go fashion. The buildings cleared and over to his right Dan caught sight of the park. Someone banged on the metal wall of the tram to alert the driver to the next stop. The passengers jostled towards the doors and spilled out on to the pavement. Dan was carried along with them.

The driver of a horse and carriage tried to block Dan's way. The man's cheeks were sunken and the ribs of the horse showed through its dusty coat. Dan dodged beneath the animal's head and walked into the park. The few carriages followed the same trail; through the gates and towards the ornamental pools. Dan ignored the drivers as they all touted for business. He walked across the bridge and into the shade given by the buildings. So impressive from a distance, many of the tiles that covered the walls were cracked and chipped. Dan sat on one of the stone benches and looked back into the heat haze that enveloped the park.

An elderly man was walking towards him, incongruously wearing a trilby hat. Dan watched him come closer, then stood up and went to offer his hand to him. The man took Dan's hand and gave him a firm handshake.

'Dan,' he said. 'It must be Dan. Let's move from here. There's a café close by.' He nodded in the direction of some trees. 'Did it take you long to get here?' he asked.

'I came by tram.'

'No, I mean the journey from Dublin.'

'Three days. Boat from Ireland, then by train through France and across Spain. Third class. No money for anything else.'

'I know what it is like. I've done it myself.'

'It was all we could afford.'

'We? You have a wife?'

'A friend,' Dan said. 'I'm travelling with a friend.'

They sat down at a small table.

'The coffee is good here. Not like in Dublin or London.'

A waiter set down two cups.

The older man said a few words to him in Spanish.

'Do you live nearby?' Dan asked.

'I live in the future,' his father said.

'I don't understand.'

'My little joke,' his father said. 'I live in Calle Porvenir. Future Street. There aren't names like that in Dublin or in London, for that matter. That's what the street is called. Future Street. So you can truthfully say my future is behind me.' He gestured over his shoulder. 'It's over there. It's not a bad place to live. Close to the stadium.'

*

'What happened?' Michael asked as Dan came into the hotel entrance hall. 'What did he say?'

'Did you get any sketching done?'

'Never mind the sketching. What happened?'

'Nothing much.'

'We've saved for twelve months. We've travelled third class halfway across Europe and you've met your father for the first time in thirty years. And all you can say is "Nothing much" when I asked you what happened.'

'We had a cup of coffee and he asked how Manchester United was getting on. The newspapers take days to get here, if they ever arrive at all.'

'That was it? Did you ask him why he left?'

'I asked and he answered.'

'And?'

'Very simple. I quote him, "Your Mother, she was a terrible one for spending the money." That's what Father said.'

'Much as you expected.'

'Mother and her ways. I don't blame the man. It must have been more than he could deal with. Football didn't bring in much money in those days.'

'And what's going to happen now?' Michael said. 'Will we stay in Seville?'

'Seville is a small place. Few foreigners come here nowadays. I'm a curiosity. To him as well as the locals. And we are going to meet tomorrow.'

'It could have been worse,' Michael said. 'Much worse. All things considered.'

Dan's Story
Seville
May 1951

'What's that?' Dan asked his father. 'There on the path and I can't work out what it is.' He put down his glass of wine and continued to watch. Something moved towards the pavement café, where the two men sat. It seemed to be a man. There was a muscular torso and well-developed arms yet where the man's legs ought to have been, was a heap of folded material. The man sank his head down into his chest in concentration and he pushed himself forward with his knuckles. He was on a small, wheeled board, a child's toy adapted for his needs. With an impressive flourish he drew up alongside the pavement café and spoke to Patrick.

'He's offering to shine your shoes.'

'They're not worth it. An old pair,' said Dan. 'Not worth the trouble.'

'A wife and four children,' Patrick said. 'He needs every centavo he can get.'

Dan turned to the man. 'It wouldn't do them any harm. Tell him to go ahead.'

Reaching behind him, the shoe-shiner took small pots out of a trailer, attached to the wooden board. The man held each pot in turn against Dan's shoes, until one met his approval. With great care, he applied the polish and set to work with a bundle of rags. Every now and again he stopped, to allow his client time to admire his handiwork.

Dan moved his shoes this way and that. The sunlight caught the newly buffed polish. 'Good,' he said. 'Very good.'

One of the waiters came over with another jug of wine and an extra glass. The shoe shiner turned his efforts to the second shoe, continuing his conversation with Patrick as he worked.

'He wants to know whether it is safe to speak in front of you.'

'A little dramatic, isn't he?'

'Can't be too careful here,' Patrick said.

'No problem at all. None. I've got half a dozen words of Spanish and no more.'

'Don't worry, I've told him you're one of us,' Patrick explained to his son. 'And I've said that you're my nephew from Dublin.'

'Is that right? I'm one of us.'

Patrick nodded.

'And I'm your nephew from Dublin.'

'Can't be too careful here.'

The waiter returned with some bread and olives. He set the food down on the table and then stood and stared at Dan.

'You're a curiosity. Foreigners are a rarity these days. Not many foreigners come to Seville.'

'No,' said Dan. 'No. I suppose they do. It took us a year to get the money together. Since your reply.'

Patrick leaned across the table. 'Have some of these,' he said and pushed the dish of olives over to Dan. 'Olives, beautiful, green olives matured with great slices of lemon and a hint of garlic. Nothing quite like them. Bread, olives and a glass of red wine. The finer things of life. What else could a man ask for?'

Patrick spat an olive stone into the palm of his hand and tossed it into the gutter. 'I don't imagine that you often get to eat olives in Dublin.'

'No,' said Dan. 'No, we don't.' He glanced down at his feet. The shoe shiner had completed his work. 'How much?' Dan asked of his father.

'A wife and four children,' Patrick repeated.

Dan reached into his pocket and took out a handful of small coins. He held them for his father to see. Patrick selected a few and set the coins down on the table. He nodded to the shoe shiner. The man picked up the remaining slices of bread and wrapped them in a piece of cloth. He then took the olives one at a time and put them into his mouth, savouring each individually. Finally, he collected together the coins.

Patrick poured him a glass of wine.

'I knew him before,' he said. 'A man of great passion.' He handed the glass to the man. The shoe shiner raised it by way of a toast and drained the contents. He then set the glass down on the edge of the table and moved off in search of another customer.

'I won't be inviting you to the house,' Patrick said. 'You do understand?'

'Naturally,' Dan said. 'I didn't expect an invitation.'

'Well,' said Patrick. 'Same time again tomorrow, if you have nothing else to do? You won't find better olives anywhere, not in all of Seville.'

Patrick's Letter from Seville
to His Brother Larry in London
November 1951

Dear Larry

Your most recent letter reached me in record time. Is it possible the censor has got bored with our communications and now only gives them a cursory glance?

It came as something of a surprise to me when I received the letter from Dan. I told you of this, I believe. The Spanish National Football Team (at last allowed out beyond the blockade and isolation in which this country is held), played in Dublin. Dan has left Manchester behind and returned to Ireland, where he now makes his home, though you possibly know this already. He went to the football match between Ireland and Spain, asked after me and was directed to Seville – as easy as that. It was unsettling to have the past rise up again. Though all this was so long ago and far behind me, I could not ignore Dan's letter or convince myself the letter had not been sent.

Ellie naturally, wanted to know in a conversational way, who it was writing to me from Ireland. It was, I believe, the first letter I had received from Dublin, in all our married life. She didn't investigate for long, but simply asked me by way of interest. 'My nephew,' I said. 'My nephew from Dublin.' She was quite content with that and merely was concerned about what she could give him to eat and to speculate on whether Dan would indeed come to visit, given the distance and the expense and if he did, would he expect to stay with us in the house or would he prefer to stay in one of the cheap hotels in the centre of the city.

As I had such warning of Dan's visit, I thought it best we meet in one of the parks. There are few foreigners here these days and they are all remarked upon as of great interest and all thought to be very rich. A park is far away from prying eyes and gossiping tongues.

So the park it was. It was difficult for me to clear my mind of the child of four or five years of age I had last seen. Now, of course, he is a man. Then, on seeing him my mind was filled with thoughts of 'his mother's looks, his mother's actions,' scarcely my son at all. Dan is most definitely his mother's son.

We got along after that first jolt. We talked of this and that. Dan is much impressed with Spain and the Spanish life, as it is his first visit abroad beyond Ireland, Scotland and England. Why he had even learned a little of the Spanish language; not enough to hold great conversations or learned discourses, but enough to find his way around and ask for a cup of coffee or a glass of wine.

For some reason Dan had got it into his head that my wife is Spanish and accepts it would be a strange situation indeed for me to present him to this woman. Dan remains 'my nephew, from Dublin,' who had little time to spend in Seville but is eager to see the sights and to move on, once he had met up with his elderly uncle.

It has to be said, Dan had set his mind to visiting me and he saved the money to make the journey. He is so unlike his mother in that respect, she was, as you know, unable to keep a shilling in her purse without suffering the irrepressible compunction to spend it.

It was encouraging to learn Dan had great interest in the Tour of Mexico and the USA, yet football is not one of his passions or even his interests. He tells me however, he has had a short story published in an American magazine and would like to visit the country at some stage in his life. On that level at least he is keen to follow my example.

It was always my fancy that if one of my children were to trace me and visit me, it would be Young Patrick. He is, I am told, living in London, caught up with worries of family and home. There will be no travelling for him. It seems I must think myself a father of four adults and no doubt, grandfather to many. Dan himself has not yet married and tells me he has no inclination to do so. Did the example of the marriage between his mother and me put him off the institution for life?

It is Dan's intention to stop off in London on his way back to Ireland. He plans to call by to see you and will, I have no doubt, fill you in on the news from Spain.

Write to me before the year is out.

Your brother,

Patrick.

The winter is fast approaching. Food is scarce, though the situation is a little better than last year. People no longer starve. An extra portion however, remains a luxury.

1952

Ellie's Letter from Seville
to Her Sister Mary in Ireland
May 1952

My Dear Mary

Is it really that long since I last wrote to you? You must forgive me.

Here once again we have lived through the ferias, the most delightful time of year in Seville. All day I have put my mind to thinking how I might best describe this magnificent event to you. Think proud men. Think women wearing dresses that hug their bodies to the hips, then tumble in full glorious flounces to their ankles. Think horsemen riding along the cobbled streets and into the parks. Think singing and dancing 'til dawn, drinking rich red wine and eating olives.

And this gives only the palest hint of what Seville is like during the ferias. This is truly the spirit of the south of Spain. If only it were possible for you to spend some time here with us. If you were ever to visit, this certainly would be the time of year to come to stay. I have to say though, it would always be a joy to see someone from home, whatever time of year.

Did I tell you a nephew of Patrick's visited us last summer? As with all young people, he was rushing around seeing the sights and, to my surprise, never came to the house to be introduced to me. It couldn't be anything but a delight to hear any news of family and friends. After all these years in Spain, it must have given Patrick no small pleasure to know that he had not been forgotten. Yet, almost before I was aware he was here, the nephew was away to the coast.

Patrick seemed to think that his nephew, Dan, was going to take a berth on one of those tramp steamers that plough up and down the Mediterranean seaboard. Given that it took three days travel to get here from Ireland, I thought he might have stayed longer, if only to let Patrick catch up on news of the nephew's mother and father. So, he has gone and Patrick is not sure whether he will come back again. There it is. Young people for you. Ever thoughtless.

What else do I have to tell you? The cost of meat remains exorbitant, though the quality of the bread is better than it has been for longer than I can remember. Soap is difficult to find in the markets. Coffee is hard to come by and is of an indifferent standard.

Patrick no longer works as a football manager, though his heart remains true to the game. Perhaps it demands too much of him at his age. He continues to scout for future talent, watching matches of the youth teams to spot the players of the future.

I've noticed him watch a match, carried away in concentration. It seems to me Patrick would have liked a son of his own. I feel sure he would have trained him as a sportsman and encouraged him to be a footballer. However, it was not to be.

Do reply soon and excuse my tardiness in writing to you. Send me some news of home.

I remain as always, your loving sister.

Ellie.

1953

Ellie's Letter from Seville
to Her Sister Mary in Ireland
June 1953

My Dear Mary

Indeed I can assure you I was very well pleased to get your letter and to have news of you and the family.

Fancy, Brigid being sixteen years old! How time flies. What is she thinking of doing? Is she still at school? What ever you do, please remember to educate them.

Every now and again I hear from Monica. In my last letter to her I mentioned that I don't intend to go to Ireland any more and that no one writes to me these days. Then, lo and behold, your letter arrived. Did Monica say something to you? It doesn't matter, either way. It was a delight to receive your letter, whatever caused you to write. I don't expect to hear from you often, as I know your hands are full with the children.

The weather is so very hot here. Even the chair I am sitting on is so uncomfortable. I touch it and it burns my hands. Can you believe it? It's impossible to eat, only drink – iced drinks. I'm positively swollen up from drinking so much water. Living here is so expensive and the poor people are very, very hungry. Coffee at 32 dollars a kilo. We can't pay in pesetas. These little coins are unacceptable for such important transactions. Incredible to believe, but it is true.

So far we have not decided what we are going to do. Whether we are going to move to England or stay in Spain. It is most likely we will go to England. Patrick is waiting for a reply to his letter to Larry.

Love to you all,

Ellie.

1954

Ellie's Letter from Seville
to Her Sister Mary in Ireland
November 1954

My Dear Mary

Very many thanks for the letter and the photographs. The children look lovely but what is wrong with them that they all wear glasses? Is this what happens to them when they study?

Fancy Brigid getting such high marks. She must be clever. Is she going into a commercial career? I am sure you will be glad when one of the children starts working.

Here it is raining the deluge. The weather isn't as in Ireland. It rains more here in one hour than in an entire day at home. The cost of living continues to trouble us. Meat that cost 1 dollar a kilo before the Civil War, now costs 12 dollars. Butter (when you can find it) that cost 2 dollars now costs 13 dollars and coffee you could get the very best for 2 dollars, now costs 30 dollars for the very worst. Everything is terribly expensive. And the wages are so low. I don't know how everything is going to end.

Enough of my complaints.

It's getting close to Christmas and I will send you a card, though they are hard to find as sending Christmas cards is not a Spanish custom. I hope this finds you and your loved ones well.

Write when you have time.

With much love,

Ellie.

1955

Patrick's Letter from Seville
to His Brother Larry in London
March 1955

Dear Larry

It is some time since I last wrote to you and, it goes without saying, I need to keep you abreast of our plans and intentions.

It is indeed a sad time for Ellie as she distributes our few possessions to friends and neighbours, as it will be necessary to leave these things behind. Thirty-two years in this country, more perhaps, thirty-three years I arrived with one suitcase and I will leave with one suitcase. Though it must be said I like to consider I have made no little mark on the world of football here in Spain. It is not excessive of me to say that football in this country would not be where it is today without my contribution.

The major event of the moment is that a mole (un topo) has been revealed here in Seville. The talk is of little else. And what is this mole? Why, he is a Red, a Republican sympathiser, no less, who had managed to remain hidden away, since the time of the Civil War. The crime of the man? He was a photographer and some of his photographs were published in a left-wing magazine – obviously a capital offence.

Every now and again, 'moles' have surfaced and it is believed in certain quarters that there are others hidden away, biding their time. For some they will re-emerge when the age of democracy arrives, for others they represent the threat that one can never escape the Communist hoards. The man was trapped when the Nationalist forces swept across the peninsula.

The man, no doubt, expected this imprisonment to be a short-term measure. The Generalísimo can't live forever though he appears to be intent on doing just that. The mole has stayed concealed for more than twenty years, waiting, avoiding capture with the assistance of his wife and one of his brothers. To no avail. I believe he would have stayed hidden away until the old despot dies or the trump of doom arrives, which ever comes first, were it not for a fire that broke out in the warren of buildings where he was hidden. He escaped the conflagration, only to be recognised and denounced by a neighbour.

Now he has been taken away for judgement (in a fair trial, in which he will be found guilty) and shot, while we are advised to be on our guard for more 'Traitors', 'Reds', 'Bolsheviks' etc. We must be thankful for the care and guidance of the Generalísimo to protect us from the foe. And the neighbour? All praise is lavished on the old crow. The man's wife and his brother await their fate.

When we return to London we will take up your offer of a place to stay, at least until we have some definite plans. Ellie favours a return to Ireland and there we take a cottage at a rent we can afford and so settle once more among our own. It has a certain attraction, though even now I have a suspicion I would not be allowed to see out my final days without some intervention from those in Manchester, should my whereabouts ever come to light.

The money arrived safely. The exchange rate was very favourable to us. The pound is high against the peseta.

I remain as ever, your brother
Patrick.

It occurs to me the post boxes in Ireland are one of the Thirty Shades of Green, those in Britain are a bright, vibrant red, while those in Spain are a dull gunmetal grey. What does this say about what this beautiful country has done to itself? Nothing has been the same since the Generalísimo came to power, even the football has suffered. Many of those who run the clubs do so because of their political beliefs, not because of their skills in the sport or their love of it. It's a sad day.

1956

Ellie's Letter from London
to Her Sister Mary in Ireland
November 1956

Dear Mary

As you will notice from the postmark we are now in London. It has been my dearest wish for some time now to spend Christmas and New Year with you all. However, it has proved impossible to get Patrick to commit himself to a date for our return, be this temporary or permanent.

You know my opinion of Larry and what a wonderful support he has been to Patrick over the years, but he can be such a bad influence as well. Together they behave like two young fellows in the big city for the first time in their lives. Only yesterday Patrick and Larry disappeared for the entire day and didn't get back to Argyle Street until late in the evening – both of them very much the worse for drink. And on occasions like this, Larry does like to sing. Even at his age his voice is still quite beautiful. For his rendition of an aria from *La Traviata* he earned himself a round of applause from one of the chambermaids, though I doubt the neighbours or the guests appreciate this at 11:30 p.m.

London is very dull after what we have been used to in Spain – the sky is rarely blue and it is so difficult to keep warm. I feel Patrick would benefit from some fresh air, especially after the smogs we have been suffering here lately. He has been having a problem with his chest, but refuses to go to see the doctor about it. If I had my way, we would rent a little cottage on the west coast of Ireland, where the air is clear and the rents are modest.

I've told Patrick if he doesn't do something about buying the tickets for the boat and sort out the journey home by the end of this month, I'm going to stay with Monica until he does.

Do not be surprised if the reply to you next letter is not from London.

As ever, your loving sister,

Ellie.

1958

Patrick's Story
London
November 1958

'There you are. I've been looking all over the house for you.'

Ellie sat very still in her armchair.

'Larry thought you might have gone out, when I couldn't find you.'

'I was sitting here,' said Ellie.

'In the dark? Let me put the light on.'

'He wasn't your nephew, was he?'

'What was that?'

'He wasn't your nephew, was he? When we were still living in Seville. It wasn't your nephew who came to visit, was it?'

Patrick sat down in the chair opposite Ellie. 'What's brought this on?'

'There weren't many Irish football managers living in Seville, as far as I know.'

'I'm not sure I'm following what you are talking about.'

'*Third Class to Seville*. He went to visit his father. He conjectures on why his father had left his mother. It was written by Dan O'Connell. He writes well. You can be proud of him.'

Patrick put his hand in his pocket and brought out a packet of cigarettes.

'She wasn't dead, was she?'

He took a cigarette out of the packet and lit it. He looked around the room for an ashtray for the dead match.

'You weren't a widower when I met you? You weren't a widower when we married, were you? She was still alive, wasn't she?' Ellie closed her eyes and took a deep breath. 'Is she still alive now?'

She stood up and went to the door. She went to open it but stood with her hand on the handle. 'If our son had been born, what would this have made him?'

She waited for a reply. 'Mary has always said there would be a place for me with her. I believe she meant if you died before me, not earlier.'

Patrick picked some loose tobacco off one of his trouser legs. He held the shred between his fingers and ran it around between them.

'Does Larry know about this? No, don't answer me. The story was in a magazine. I came across it in the guests' lounge. I suspect Larry's fancy bit had something to do with it. My finding the magazine, I mean. Left it there for me to discover. She's never liked me. I've never liked her, for that matter and now I find I'm no better than she is.'

Patrick opened his mouth to speak but then decided against it.

'I've got some of my things together. I'll collect the rest in the morning. I hope you'll come to the station to see me off, but you don't have to.'

Ellie opened the door to the hallway. 'I thought I knew you, Patrick,' she said. 'I thought I knew you.'

Patrick's Story
London
November 1958

'You get to see life in this job.' The young clerk dropped some files onto his desk.

'What's that?' his colleague asked.

'That old bloke. Been in again. You know, the one I told you about.'

The clerk's colleague leaned over the desk to get a better look at the contents of the folder. 'Never heard of him,' he said.

'You mightn't've but my granddad has.'

'Oh, yes?'

'Played with Clapton Orient, Leyton Orient as was. Manchester United, at some stage. Quite a star in his time.'

'When's that then?'

'First World War. Around then. Captained United and Ireland, my granddad said.'

'What's he been doing since?'

'Abroad.' The clerk ran his finger down his notes. 'Spain. There it is. He's been living in Spain.' The clerk pointed out the information to his colleague.

'Who'd he play for there?

'Didn't play there. Too old by then – to play professional standard, I mean. No, he managed some of their best teams. Top rank.'

Another man joined the conversation. 'It was in the Irish papers. I remember the name. It catches your attention with a surname like that among the Spanish teams. Manager of one or two of them. He was on tour. South America, if I remember.'

'He's been there all this time?'

'No. Went back to Spain. Told me which teams he had managed.'

The young clerk began ticking the teams off on his fingers, ending with 'and FC Barcelona.'

His colleague whistled through his teeth in appreciation of the list. 'Get away.'

'Honest.'

One of the secretaries glanced up from her work, a pained expression on her face. 'If you must talk about football,' she said, 'at least talk about it grammatically.'

The young clerk turned in her direction. 'Yes, honestly,' he said, with emphasis.

'What's he doing now? Must be getting on a bit. Where'd he live?'

The young clerk looked at the file again. 'The Avoca Hotel. That's where he lives.'

'What does he want National Assistance for if he can afford to live in a hotel?' his colleague asked.

'It's one of those run-down places off the Euston Road. It belongs to his brother and his brother can't afford to keep him.'

'It's a bit rich, isn't it? Coming back here after all this time and wanting to claim National Assistance.'

'He's got an attic room at his brother's hotel.'

'Give you his life history, did he?

The young clerk continued to read through his notes. 'He was an interesting kind of bloke,' he said. 'Imagine coming back to all this, after all the glories of the pitch and the sun of Spain.'

The men turned to look out of the grime-covered windows onto the traffic of the Euston Road.

'It must have been a bit of a shock for him,' said one of them.

1959

'It has to be said, life has been good to me. Who has had the opportunity to do what I have done? Who indeed.'

The young nurse nodded.

'From the very beginning it was the football. Larry and I from the time we first were able to walk, we played. It kept us bright through school and when the lads came pouring out of that dreadful building at the end of the day, it was the football that raised our spirits. Larry gave up the game when he realised he couldn't beat me. I would always win. It took me further than most, I grant you. Beyond the back streets of Dublin and the banks of the Liffey. It took me halfway across Europe and halfway across the world.

'The move to England, a goal in the first match at Manchester United, managing Betis de Sevilla to the top of the First Division to win *La Liga*, doing whatever possible to save FC Barcelona from bankruptcy in the dark days of the Spanish Civil War. What more might a man want?'

The elderly man coughed and clutched a handkerchief to his mouth.

'You would be better concentrating on getting better,' said the nurse. 'Never mind all this about football and your life in detail.'

The elderly man went on with his story, undetered by her comments.

'The Ellen of my youth; how she could spend the money. The foolish behaviour of the early years – one mistake and you are married and a child is on the way – I always knew she would be able to manage, to survive. I knew she would get by, better for both of us in every way. She never starved. Not much I grant you, though I sent her what I was able.

'The Ellie of my later years, a good woman, a caring woman, always put my interests above her own. Fortune brought her to me. It was a great pity at the end, but that couldn't be helped at all.

'Life has been good to me, in a very singular way.'

Patrick's Story
St Pancras Hospital, London
February 1959

'Take it away, will you? Take it away. Go on.'

The young nurse did as she was told.

'Never have understood and never will. A plate of stewed prunes and the people in this country think they've a great delicacy set down before them. Put custard on it and they believe they've been given the very ambrosia of the gods. Go on. Take it away. I've no stomach for it.'

The nurse put the plate on the trolley and went back to the bedside. 'Will you be having visitors this afternoon, Mr O'Connell?' she asked.

Patrick didn't give any indication he had heard.

'The time. What time did you say it was? Thought it was later. There's a watch in there somewhere.'

The nurse opened the drawer. She rummaged around in it.

'Right there. That's it. Can't reach it myself. If I'm not asking too much of you. Get the watch out for me, will you? Leave it there. A little to the left. That's it. Can see it myself then. Without having to trouble anyone.'

The nurse put the watch on the bedside cupboard.

'Don't tell me. Larry says the same, every visit. "Let me take it home with me, Patrick, I'll be taking the watch with me. It isn't as if you need it when you are in the hospital. A watch like that in here and the next moment somebody will have gone off with it. Wait and see. You wait."

'Your brother might be right, Mr O'Connell,' said the nurse.

Her patient continued his one sided conversation. 'Says it every time. Every time he comes in. Old fool that I am, but I don't let him take it. That's how it is. Had that watch with me how long? An age now. Wouldn't feel right, no, if I've not got it with me. Doesn't feel right. But there it is. Without it, I don't feel right. That's how it is. "Yes," says Larry, "And when someone's gone off with it, what are you going to do then? Let me put it in your suitcase with all your other things, that'll be for the best. You can have it when you come back to stay with me." Says the same thing every visit.'

Patrick coughed. With difficulty, he turned towards the nurse. 'What time did you say it was? Is that all? Move the watch a little. That's right. Light was shining on the face. Couldn't see it. That's better. Larry's due here at half past.'

The nurse looked at her watch. 'I must go,' she said.

'Says he'll be in to visit this afternoon. Doesn't like to drive after dark. Afternoons are better for him. Says his eyesight isn't what it used to be. He'll be here soon. It breaks up the day. To have a visitor. Larry. A good brother. Always been a good brother. One of the best, if you want to know.'

The nurse nodded and moved off to attend to another patient.

The elderly man continued with his conversation with no one in particular. 'The scraps we got in to. When we were young. Always been close. One of the best, is Larry. Would be the right thing. To leave the watch to Larry, that is. To say I'd appreciated what he's done for me. Over the years. Not that he needs it. Done better than any of us. Done better than all the rest of us put together. A hotel or two and a car. Larry's done nicely for himself. No, he doesn't need anything. Not Larry. Leave it to him to say I've appreciated what he's done for me. That's all. A gesture.'

The young nurse hurried back to the elderly man's bedside. She pulled the curtains around the bed as she moved.

'A terrible thing. And not pleasant for you.'

'That's alright,' she said. 'I'll go and get the doctor. Back in one moment.'

'Nothing I could do about it. No warning. Draw the curtain. That's it. Round here. That's better. It's the lungs. The lungs're worn out. All that breathing. All those years. And Larry. What does he say? "What about the flour?" Could see the flour. Hanging there. In the air. Could taste it, you could. The flour. Even before it was baked. Boland's.'

The nurse came back to the elderly man's bedside, unaware the conversation had continued without her.

'Boland's. Critical, it was. In the uprising.'

'Never mind about that just now. The doctor will be here in a moment.'

'The uprising. 1916. We were young and full of hope.'

'When was that?'

'1916. It was 1916.'

Curiosity overcame her professionalism.

'There was I thinking you lived in England.'

'I did, yes but I went home from time to time. We knew something was afoot. The uprising was going to happen.'

'And you were there?'

The elderly man coughed again. The cough wracked his body.

'There. I knew you ought to be waiting quietly for the doctor.'

'Plenty of time for being quiet.'

'What happened? My father would be interested, for sure.'

'I could drive,' said Patrick, 'And that was not something you could depend upon in those days. Now every young man has set his sights on a car. Working in Ford's in the summer and I learned to drive. The lorries and the vans and the trucks and that was how we got the supplies around. Too heavy to carry and a lot of risk, though the young women were good at that.'

'What was that?' asked the nurse.

'Hid the guns in their petticoats.'

'Did they now?'

'And so they did. In the folds of their skirts and in amongst their petticoats.'

The nurse busied herself with the clip chart from the end of the bed. She looked up. 'Really. Is that so?'

'Oscar knew I could drive. He knew. Went on to great things in the new government. The Free State Government. And him a footballer. Ought to have been Minister for Sport but no, Telephones and Posts or something like that.'

The nurse assured Patrick that the doctor was due there in a moment.

Patrick spoke to the young nurse again. 'You know Boland's Mill, don't you?' She made a non-commital comment. 'That's where it was. The mill. Boland's. First job. Fifty years ago. No. More. More than fifty years ago. A long time. Before your mammy and your dah were born I suspect. That young fellow. The one who comes round each morning. Looks too young to be a doctor. Told him about the flour. All he said was "Cigarettes". Doesn't matter now. Not now. Too late for all that.'

The nurse plumped up the pillows for the elderly man. He leaned back again. 'Could do with a smoke. Larry'll bring a packet for me. Can rely on it. He remembers. Cigarettes. One of dark tobacco, one of light tobacco.'

'Smoking is only allowed in the Visitors' Room,' said the nurse. Patrick didn't appear to have heard.

'They all knew me for that, the footballers. The footballers. I told you I'd been a footballer?'

The young nurse nodded. 'Several times,' she said.

'One of each. One cigarette of dark tobacco, one of light. Told the footballers not to smoke. "Do what I say, not what I do." *Stukka*, they called him *Stukka*. His nickname. After the fighter plane, the Nazi one. Small and fast. I wouldn't let him play after I caught him smoking. Banned him for a game or two. Never smoked again. Not in his entire life, I've heard. Made an impression on the young fellows. Best way to get in the team. Follow my guiding light. And what teams I've managed. None better. Manchester United – played for them, was the Captain – and FC Barcelona – managed them – none better.'

The nurse patted the pillow and went off to attend to another patient. 'Doctor will be here in a moment,' she said as she went.

'Light tobacco; less harsh. Dark tobacco; more economic. Home grown in Spain. Fields of the stuff. Growing all over the place. Could see it from the window of the train. Where was it we were going? Can't remember. It'll come to me in a moment. Can't remember now. Somewhere in Spain. When the young fellows and I, the team and I, used to travel to the matches. The football games. A long time ago.'

The elderly man woke with a start. He spoke again to no one in particular. 'Must have been dozing. Larry'll be here soon. Doesn't like to drive in the dark. Not these days. Says the traffic bothers him. Doesn't need the watch. Not Larry. He's got more than enough. Ought to go to Young Patrick. The watch. Him being the eldest. By rights, it ought to be his. Won't even remember who I am. Young Patrick won't even remember who I am. His old dah. Not now. Won't remember. Too late. All gone.'

The man in the next bed to Patrick rang for the nurse.

'All behind me now. All behind me. Larry'll be here soon. Think I'll have a little nap. Before he gets here. Just a few moments. A doze before Larry gets here.'

The nurse arrived at the bedside and turned off the buzzer.

'I think he's on his way out,' the man in the next to Patrick said. 'You'll need to get the doctor.'

Ellie's Letter from London
to Her Sister Mary in Ireland
February 1959

Dear Mary

Patrick is dead. He died before I got back to London. I am bereft. He died in the hospital yesterday.

Patrick *Requiescat In Pacem*.

Write to me.

Your loving sister,

Ellie.

Larry's Story
Argyle Street, Kings Cross, London
March 1959

'It's all I could let him have,' said Larry. 'It's not Seville, but at least he had a roof over his head.' He sat down in the armchair. Dan sat on the bed. 'Ellie and Lilly don't get on, you know. When your father was here on his own there was no trouble. Like the old days. But when his wife joined him, it was different altogether.'

Dan pulled the suitcase out from under the bed.

'Is this it?' he asked.

'Everything. You will find everything in there.'

Dan began lifting out the clothes. At the bottom of the suitcase was a layer of newspaper cuttings. Larry picked up a handful and began looking through them. A few fluttered to the floor.

'Look at this, will you, "Don Patricio O'Connell." Your father was a very Spanish man. Irish and proud of it but Spanish as well.'

Larry held out a sheet of paper to Dan.

'What is it?' the young man asked.

'This would be the training certificate. 1950, 1951 – around then, if I remember. Your father qualified as a football manager.'

'Isn't that what he had been doing for thirty years?'

'Everybody had to have their papers in order. Mountains of the stuff. Forms to be completed in triplicate ... to blow your nose. Official documents for everything. That's what your father said.'

Dan shook his head.

'There's no watch in here.'

'Didn't I tell him,' said Larry, 'not to keep it with him in the hospital, but no, he wouldn't listen. That was your father for you.' He leaned back in the chair and massaged one of his knees. 'This weather doesn't do me any good. Not at my age. Didn't do your father any good either. You are certain it isn't in there?'

Dan shook his head again. 'Papers. Photographs. Can't see anything else.' He passed some photographs to Larry to look through.

'You see this?' said Larry. 'There's your father.' He pointed to a photograph of a bald man standing amongst a group of young men.

'The Real Betis team. When they won the first division, *La Liga*, with your father as manager. He's still revered in Seville to this day, I believe, though it was ... let me see.' He turned the photograph over and read what was written on the back. 'Yes, the 1934/35 season when they won the trophy. Will you look at it?'

Dan took the offered photograph. 'Do you mind if I keep it?' he asked.

Larry shook his head. 'What will I be doing with it? No, you keep it. It's yours. I'll be getting downstairs. Your father's wife will be here within the hour. Come down and join us, when you are ready. We'll take a drop of whiskey before we go. It's what we need when we go to bury a father and a brother. God rest his soul.'

Larry got to his feet. Dan went on sifting through the remaining photographs: his father standing behind a display of trophies, his father wearing shorts and a jersey standing on the pitch with a group of unknown footballers, his father sitting on a bench in a sports stadium wearing a suit and a trilby hat.

'Vanity,' Larry said, looking over Dan's shoulder. 'He wore that hat, even in the baking heat of Spain, so people wouldn't know he was bald. Would you credit it, in all that heat? A trilby hat.'

'He was wearing his hat when I met him,' said Dan. 'I didn't realise he wore it all the time. It must have been so uncomfortable, in that heat.'

Larry picked up a pair of pyjamas from the bed.

'I'll take these. They were mine to begin with.' He folded the nightclothes over his arm.

'If you want to stay the night, this room is free. Your father won't be wanting it now.'

Patrick's Obituary
in the *Catalan Sportsman*, Barcelona
April 1959

News has reached us of the untimely death of the renowned football manager Mister Patrick O'Connell. He had lately returned to London to live with his brother, after a long and illustrious career here in Spain.

Patrick O'Connell arrived in Spain in 1922 after playing for some of the most noted of English clubs; namely Sheffield Wednesday, Hull City and Manchester United, where he was Captain at the time of the 1914–1918 War. Mister O'Connell also returned to his birth place from time to time to captain his national team of Ireland.

Patrick O'Connell brought to Spain a level of football skills fresh to this country. His untiring work set down the foundations of some of our greatest clubs and helped make them what they are today. He most surely was the first in the world of football to realise that good defence comes before attack. Patrick O'Connell brought this basic rule as an innovation to our country. Football was the stronger for his work.

Patrick O'Connell's managerial work saw Racing de Santander gain entry to the First Division in 1929. His move to Real Betis de Sevilla was highlighted when the Team won La Liga for the 1934–1935 season, the only occasion to date. From here Patrick O'Connell moved to FC Barcelona. Despite this being a time of great troubles for the people of this country Patrick O'Connell managed the team to further successes, most notably as runner up in the Campeonato de Catalunia in 1936 and the winner of the Liga Mediterránea the following year. Later that same year of 1937 Patrick O'Connell managed the Team on the Tour of Mexico and the USA, effectively saving FC Barcelona from bankruptcy.

Had the history of this country been different, who can imagine to what heights Patrick O'Connell would have risen and where he might have taken our National Team.

Not only did Patrick O'Connell bring a new approach to the game but he also brought football training methods to this country that were trend setting – he wasn't afraid of putting on his shorts and a jersey and getting out on the pitch – something now taken for granted, though new at the time.

Tales told by footballers now retired from the sport indicate that Patrick O'Connell even had an influence on the Spanish language. As our readers will know all football managers in this country are known as 'el mister'; it is said that this came about in honour of Mr Patrick O'Connell, so great has been his influence on the sport. The English word has been adopted to refer to all football managers.

Saturday Next at the Camp Nou
Two Minutes Silence Will Be Held In Memory of
One of Our Greatest Football Managers
Mister Patrick O'Connell.

1960

Young Patrick's Story
King's Cross, London
April 1960

Two men came out of the Underground at St Pancras' Station. They crossed the Euston Road and turned into one of the side streets.

'Are you certain then, he'll still be living here?' the younger man asked.

'I am. I am,' the older man replied. The narrow street was lined with small hotels. The two men walked along reading the names on the signs, in the hope one would spark a memory.

'This is it. This will be the one,' the older man said. 'Larry must be living here. It's certain he'll be living here.'

The younger man looked at the building. 'You remembered it?'

'This will be the hotel. The Avoca. We always used to go there, to Avoca, from Dublin. It will be "The Avoca: The Meeting of the Waters".'

A woman opened the door. 'We full. No room,' she said. 'Try along street.'

'It's not a room we are looking for,' the older man said. 'It is Mr O'Connell we've called to see. Mr Laurence O'Connell, Larry. Is he here just now?'

'I look.'

'I am his nephew. His nephew, Patrick,' the older man said.

'Moment,' the woman replied and retreated into the darkness of the entrance hall. She left the two men standing at the half open door. The younger man looked at the older man.

'Wonder who she might be?'

Patrick didn't answer.

'What Larry has to tell you, Dad, might not be what you want to hear. You do know that, don't you?'

'I do, son. I do.'

The younger man looked around, his attention caught by a sudden noise. An elderly man had opened a ground floor window and put his head out.

'Patrick. Hello, Patrick,' he shouted across to the two men who waited on the doorstep. 'I'll be with you in a moment. It's good to see you. It's been too long.' He disappeared from sight and a moment later he flung open the main door of the hotel.

Larry looked at the younger man.

'This is my son,' said Patrick.

'Won't you be coming in? Let's all go up to the sitting room. Best room in the house.' Larry guided the two men along the corridor and up the stairs. 'Go on up to the first floor. You'll find more light gets to the first floor.'

The two men were ushered into a large room at the front of the building. The woman was already there. She sat at a desk, sorting through some papers. She got to her feet. 'You like tea? No trouble.'

'Lilly,' said Larry, by way of introduction. 'She makes a lovely cup of tea. A great help, in every way.'

Larry settled himself on the chair vacated by Lilly. The visitors sat on the sofa.

'Well,' said Larry. 'It's good to see you again. Patrick. It must have been an age. And it's great to meet young Michael again.'

'This isn't Michael,' Patrick said. 'This is Patrick, Patrick Kevin. My son Michael isn't here just now. He's living away. Recently married, I believe. This is my son, Patrick Kevin.'

'Patrick Kevin,' Larry repeated. The two men turned to look at the young man. 'It's great to meet you ... to see you both. After an age. It is.'

Steps were heard on the stairs.

'Lilly with the tea,' said Larry.

Patrick Kevin left his father sitting on the sofa. He opened the door into the hallway. Lilly carried the tray into the room and set it down on the desk. Larry glanced at the four cups and saucers. Lilly smiled. 'You excuse me. Hundred things to do.'

'A great help around the business. It's more than I can be doing now, at my age. A great help.'

The older man stirred a second spoon of sugar into his cup. 'I am here ... that is ... I've come here today ... the two of us ... ' He took a sip of his of tea. 'What can you tell me about my father? I've been thinking about him. Time and time again, I find I come back to him. It's always in my mind. I'd like to know where he is.'

'Well now,' Larry said. 'Your father. Now, would you be taking a drop of whiskey in your tea?' He stood up and rummaged in the desk. From beneath a pile of papers, he pulled out a half-empty bottle.

'Yes,' he said. 'Your father.'

He poured generous measures of the whiskey into each of the teacups. The visitors watched him.

'Either way, I have to know … good or bad. Whatever it is. I have to know.'

Larry took a drink. 'He left Spain,' he said. 'You did know that?'

'I didn't.'

'He was here for a while, a short time. Not for long.'

'We live in Plaistow,' the older man said. 'It isn't far from here.'

'No,' said Larry. 'No. It isn't far. A few miles.'

'And now? Where is he now? Gone to Ireland? Gone back to Spain? Where is he now?'

The younger man interrupted. 'Dad has always wanted to see his father again. Is he still in London? Where is he?'

Larry swilled the tea around in the cup. He looked at it with great attention. 'He's in Kensal Green'. He took another sip of the tea.

'Kensal Green?'

'He was in the hospital. Not for long. A few days. But now he's, well, I have to say, he's in the cemetery in Kensal Green. Since early last year. The pneumonia took him.'

'We didn't know that.'

Larry continued to look into his teacup. 'The pneumonia took him. Wouldn't do what the doctors said. Weak lungs … and the flour and the cigarettes didn't help at all.'

The older man agreed. 'No,' he said. 'Those wouldn't help at all.'

Larry raised his cup. 'To Patrick,' he said.

'To Patrick,' said both the visitors, getting to their feet.

'A brother without equal. May he rest in peace.'

They drained their teacups and set them down on the saucers.

*

Patrick Kevin and his father walked back towards the underground station.

'What did Larry say again?' the older man asked. 'I didn't quite hear. I was distracted.'

'His wife came back with him from Spain. She left him on the station. They parted on the station and she went south. That's all Larry would say … and he showed me a letter, but it was written in Spanish.'

'She went south. The south of Ireland? The south of London? Where?'

'Don't know. No idea. Larry wouldn't say.'

'And Larry didn't mention the watch?'

'No,' said the younger man. 'He did not.'

The younger man grabbed his father by the arm and pulled him back from the kerb. 'Mind where you are going, Dad. You'll be getting yourself killed like that, if you're not more careful. Didn't you see?'

The older man blinked. 'No. What was it? What's the matter?'

They continued along the Euston Road and turned towards the entrance to the Underground.

'Do you want to go to Kensal Green?'

'And you said his wife "went south"?'

'That's all Larry would say. She had gone south. South of Ireland. South of London. Back to Spain. Don't know. Larry wouldn't say. Just that they had parted on the railway station and that she had gone south ... and he showed me a letter ... but it was written in Spanish.'

'I didn't know he was here.'

'No,' the younger man said. 'No. You didn't know. None of us knew.'

'I would have liked to have seen him again. Just once. I would have liked to have done that.'

'I know, Dad. I do know.'

'Did she ... his wife ... go to his funeral?'

'Larry didn't say. What he did tell me was that Dan got over from Dublin, for the funeral, that is. He got over from Ireland to go to the funeral.'

'Well now,' the older man said. 'Dan went to the funeral and he didn't say anything to me, to any of us, about it ... but that's Dan for you.'

They walked down the steps to the Underground.

The older man got some coins out of his pocket. He counted them into the palm of his hand. 'Have you any more money for the ticket machines?' he said. 'I've changed my mind. We're going to Kensal Green.'

And Afterwards

Ellen's Obituary
in the *Manchester Evening Post*
13 June 1983

As written by her daughter Nell

O'Connell (Ellen) née Treston

On 12 June 1983 at home, aged 96 years. Ellen dearly loved wife of the late Patrick and loving mother of Nell and Dan and the late Patrick and Nancy and dear mother-in-law of Tom, a much loved grandmother and great grandmother. Service and committal at Blackley Crematorium on Friday, June 17th at 12 noon.

Ellie's Obituary
Ireland
June 1995

Ellen O'Connell (née O'Callaghan) 1895–1995

The death of Ellie O'Connell has taken place in her 100th year.

Ellie was much travelled and had lived in France and later in Spain for a good part of her life. She first went to France as nanny to the children of a British diplomatic family and then moved with the family to Spain. Once there, Ellie moved in the highest circles, mixing with Royalty and with the International Diplomatic Corps.

Traditionally, each summer the Spanish Court and their entourage would move from the oppressive heat of Madrid to the more equitable climes of the city of Santander, on the Bay of Biscay. Ellie's work meant that she moved with her young charges.

It was in Santander that Ellie first met Patrick O'Connell, who was at the time Manager of the football team FC Racing de Santander. They married a little before the outbreak of the Spanish Civil War and continued in Spain for much of their lives together.

In July 1936 at the outbreak of the Spanish Civil War, the couple was fortunate to have been enjoying their annual summer holidays in Ireland. They took the decision to return to the country they both loved and remained in Barcelona for a large part of the Civil War.

As Franco's troops swept north and Nationalist victory was certain, Ellie was evacuated on a British Navy frigate and Patrick managed to escape overland. The couple delighted in telling of their chance reunion on the steps of the Spanish Emergency Committee buildings in London.

Patrick's career took him back to Spain in the early 1940s. The couple moved around the country depending on where Patrick was offered his next managerial post. On his retirement the couple settled once again in the delightful Andalucian city of Seville.

Patrick and Ellie finally left Spain in late 1954. They moved back to London, where one of Patrick's brothers kept a small hotel.

After Patrick's death in 1959, Ellie spent some years working as a companion to various lady dowagers. Her skills were much in demand as she had moved in court circles and understood court etiquette. Ellie also had a fine command of French and Spanish.

In the 1970s Ellie moved back to Ireland and spent her final days close to her family.

To the couple's great sadness there were no children to the marriage.

The Children of Patrick O'Connell and Ellen Treston

Patrick O'Connell, eldest son and namesake of the footballer Patrick O'Connell, moved from Manchester to London during the Second World War. He worked in the National Fire Service and later for London Underground.

His wife, Nancy Manuel, moved to be with him after the war was over.

Throughout his life, Patrick continued to look for his father. Until the day he died, Patrick regretted that he never saw his father again after the family left Dumbarton in 1919.

Patrick had, however, learned little from his experience and abandoned his eldest son. His eldest son Michael was left in Manchester to be raised by his grandmother, Ellen Treston, and his Aunt Nell and her husband Tom. Patrick never made any effort to get his son back to live with his birth parents and siblings. Patrick, son of Patrick, never did start the revolution.

Patrick died in 1972.

Patrick O'Connell's daughter Nancy briefly found her prince and spent much of the remainder of her life raising her children and working as a seamstress. She died in 1976.

Patrick O'Connell's daughter Nell worked as a secretary and went on to become a regular radio broadcaster in England in the 1950s and 1960s, with stories of her Irish childhood in Manchester. The last surviving child of Patrick O'Connell and Ellen Treston, she died aged ninety on 8 March 2005, 118 years after the birth of her father.

Patrick O'Connell's son Dan returned to Ireland shortly before the outbreak of the Second World War. He became a successful actor and playwright. For many years Dan worked at the Gate Theatre, Dublin, on stage and later as a director. In 1963 he won the prestigious Prix Italia for his play *Piano in the Liffey* and went on to have his own radio programme on RTE. After his retirement, Dan worked for the gay rights movement in Ireland. Dan died in 1995.

Other than Dan, none of Patrick O'Connell's children saw their father after the family left Dumbarton in 1919.

*

The Dazzler, who appears in this book, is the eldest grandson of the footballer Patrick O'Connell and his first wife, Ellen Treston. He, as all six of Patrick O'Connell's grandchildren, was to get divorced. The Dazzler remarried and his new wife wrote this book. As she worked on it, she came to forgive Patrick O'Connell for the damage he caused to the family he left behind and to so many other people.

Patrick O'Connell's football career was exceptional, but was won at a certain cost.

It is the wish of the writer of this book that it serve as a memorial to a truly extraordinary man. Patrick O'Connell was an outstanding sportsman, but as a husband and a father he was a non-starter.

It is the writer's intention that Patrick O'Connell be rescued from oblivion.

Acknowledgements

This book has been a true pleasure to research and write. Along the way I have met and been helped by many kind and thoughtful people who have given their time and energy to help me put together a more complete picture of Patrick O'Connell.

In particular, I would like to thank the late Nell and Tom Holmes. Nell had a wealth of stories about her father and was always prepared to share them with me.

In Ireland, I would like to express my particular thanks to Fergus Dowd, Alan McLean and Simon Needham, who have so successfully promoted the Patrick O'Connell Memorial Fund and who have who have found themselves so caught up in the life of Patrick O'Connell that they have succeeded in bringing Patrick O'Connell into the consciousness of the people of Ireland. Joining this trio has been Maureen O'Sullivan, TD for Drumcondra, Dublin, who, despite a heavy workload, has worked tirelessly to promote Patrick. Together they have done so much to promote a suitable memorial to the man.

As Patrick began his professional football career more than 100 years ago, nobody survives from his early professional days. However, I would like to thank the management and supporters, too numerous to mention by name, of the clubs where Patrick O'Connell either played or managed.

In Barcelona, I would like to give particular thanks to Sr Josep Maria Bartomeu, President of FC Barcelona, for the help he offered.

In Seville, I would like to thank Vitorio Duque de Seras, a mad keen Bético, who guided us around the places where Patrick had lived and introduced us to people he had known, as well as members of the club administration and supporters of FC Real Bétis de Sevilla, who made us feel so at home.

In Santander, I would like to thank Rául Gomez Sampero and Jóse Manuel Muñoz of FC Racing de Santander.

Thanks also to the supporters of the smaller clubs: in Ireland the supporters of FC Liffey Wanderers who sing so well; in Scotland to the supporters of

Dumbarton FC; and in England, those of Ashington FC were amazing in the amount of help they were able to offer.

Then, there are so many journalists and writers who have put so much energy and effort into aiding me with my researches – whether they be Spanish, Catalan, Scottish, Mexican, English or Irish. I thank them so much.

I would like to express my appreciation for the support and input of Mike Hunt and Christine Johnson, Mike Martin and Dr Jack Orchison. This is a small group of mainly published authors. We have met regularly over several years. They have analysed my work minutely and have come up with constructive advice, all along the line, for which I have been truly grateful.

Further, I would also like to mention the invaluable help given by Mark Wylie, Curator of Manchester United Museum and Tour Centre, along with the great help offered by the archivists of FC Barcelona.

There are so many others to thank. These include Nigel Holland, Principal of Holland and Company, who so scrupulously managed the financial affairs of the Patrick O'Connell Memorial Fund without remunerative consideration. He is an avid follower of Patrick O'Connell.

Also, thanks must go to the staff of the National Newspaper Archives at Colindale, London, who offered me assistance as they sought out newspapers and microfiches to help me. Thanks to the staff at the Public Records Office at Kew, London, who offered similar assistance.

Above all I would like to thank my husband Mike O'Connell, a grandson of Patrick O'Connell. He didn't realise what he was unleashing when he first introduced me, on a bus in Madrid, to the few stories that were then known about Patrick. It goes without saying that without him, none of this would have been possible.